The G Quotient

Why Gay Executives Are Excelling as Leaders . . .

and What Every Manager Needs to Know

Kirk Snyder

JOSSEY-BASS
A Wiley Imprint
www.josseybass.com

Published by Jossey-Bass
A Wiley Imprint
989 Market Street, San Francisco, CA 94103-1741   www.josseybass.com

Library of Congress Cataloging-in-Publication Data

Snyder, Kirk.
    The G quotient : why gay executives are excelling as leaders—and what every manager needs to know / Kirk Snyder.
        p. cm.
    Includes bibliographical references and index.
    ISBN 978-1-118-43898-5
    1. Leadership. 2. Executives. 3. Gay men. I. Title.
HD57.7.S688 2006
658.4'092—dc22   2006009302

FIRST EDITION
HB Printing   10 9 8 7 6 5 4 3 2 1

Contents

Preface

Many years ago, while I was studying the art of entrepreneurship as an undergraduate at the University of Southern California, the late Marcia Israel—one of the most successful self-made women in the history of the retail field—told my class that good entrepreneurs see *connection* where others see disconnection. Whether or not I'm a good entrepreneur is a chapter in my life that's still being written. However, what I will take credit for at this point is connecting several observable realities in the newly recalibrated world of work and following what has been an uncharted path in the study of business leadership.

Over a period of five years, my research for *The G Quotient* spanned more than three thousand working professionals, representing an expansive cross-section of diverse organizations from California to North Carolina to The Netherlands. (For more detail about this research, please see Appendix B.)

Initially, my main goal for this project was to identify specific leadership behaviors that the next generation of managers would need to embrace in order to achieve and sustain career success over the next decade. Along the way, I recognized one of those entrepreneurial connections, and the project took an unexpected turn in a very different direction. As a result of my detour, I created a new phase of research and subsequently surveyed more than a thousand employees (across four major U.S. business sectors: Fortune 500 companies, colleges and universities, government, and small business) working under the leadership of gay male executives, referred to throughout this book simply as "gay executives." Consisting of primarily straight employees, this new research established a positive correlation between the leadership behaviors evidenced in organizations managed by these gay executives and the significantly higher-than-average rates of job engagement, satisfaction, and workplace morale reported by their employees. Ultimately, this new phase of research provided the title for this book by putting the "G" in *The G Quotient*, resulting in what some cautioned was a leadership book too controversial to be published.

Making the Connection

From 2003 through 2004, I studied (empirically as well as through field research) what I will refer to throughout this book as the *reconstruction of contemporary employees*. Without getting too far ahead of myself, the practical implication of this new term is essentially a recalibration of employee beliefs, values, and expectations. It's also a primary contributor to the leadership success of gay executives—and therefore an important part of *The G Quotient*. A natural by-product of what is often referred to as the Digital Age, the world itself gave today's employees their key tool for reinvention—instant access to specialized, work-related *knowledge*.

Along with the reconstruction of contemporary employees, the meaning of successful leadership has been simultaneously and unavoidably recalibrated as well. The end result is a message that resonates across a diverse spectrum of business playing fields from the Fortune 500 to entrepreneurial enterprises in virtually all fields and industries. Today's workforce is the most knowledgeable, diverse, and empowered in recorded history, and old leadership paradigms no longer apply. Why? Because the business world they originally served no longer exists.

Defining the G Quotient

While corporate America is seemingly baffled by the steady decline in across-the-board levels of employee engagement, job satisfaction, and workplace morale, employees under the leadership of gay exec-

The following chart details the percentages of employees who report higher levels of job engagement, job satisfaction, and workplace morale under the leadership of gay male managers, compared with nationally reported statistics. (For more detail on the G Quotient results, see Appendix D.)

	G Quotient	Nationally
Engagement	85.30	21[1]
Job satisfaction	81.39	45[2]
Workplace morale	84.82	40[3]

utives in the four major business sectors I studied are the collective exception. In all four sectors, employees in these environments report significantly higher levels of job engagement, job satisfaction, and workplace morale than comparative national averages.

My research found that in organizations and working units under the direct leadership of non-closeted gay executives, an environment is created where employees care about their work, demonstrate a deep commitment to professional excellence, and feel individually connected to advancing the success of the organization itself. Because these executives approach their leadership role with a worldview that places primary value on the individual, they believe each employee has the right to a place of foremost importance within the organization. This belief fosters a workplace climate based on a foundation of inclusion, which in turn breeds a type of employee engagement rarely seen in other professional environments.

What makes G Quotient leadership different? When leadership is based on absolute inclusion, meaning that all employees are viewed by their managers as having the value and authority to play a key role in the success of the organization because of who they are as human beings, it cements a positive, equality-based connection between employees and their managers. Without this type of authentic personal connection, today's employees will typically disengage from their work because they feel their employers view them simply as laborers rather than as fully participating and meaningful *contributors* to the organization.

Getting Over the "G" Word

Do you have to be a gay male to be a G Quotient leader?

Absolutely not.

G Quotient leaders come in all mixes of gender and sexual orientation. (See Appendix C for the range of G Quotient scores among various demographic groups.)

However, because this is the first business leadership book of its kind—based on the first large-scale research of its kind—I believe it's necessary to further address the "G" word and the role sexual orientation does or does not play in G Quotient leadership.

The G Quotient is not a gay management style. However, for a variety of reasons explored in detail in the Introduction, gay executives are in the right place at the right time to achieve beyond the status quo as business leaders. Several phenomena combine to explain the development of G Quotient leadership among this particular group of professionals: employee needs, learned social skills, and the convergence of documented sociocultural factors and trends. As identified in my research, it's a group that, as a collective whole, face no additional types of oppression other than their sexual orientation. Primarily white, middle-class, and college-educated, these gay executives bridge the traditional world of business, historically run by straight white males, and the new business world where diversity, creativity, and empathy are viewed as professional commodities.

In Part One of this book, you will meet the namesakes of G Quotient leadership, and later, many of their employees. It's important to note that for the purposes of my research, the gay executives identified throughout this book all carry out their leadership roles in friendly and affirming environments and are non-closeted in their professional lives. Listed at the end of this Preface, the organizations they serve range from global household names to government agencies and successful entrepreneurial business enterprises.

In Part Two, I delve more deeply into the reasons why G Quotient leadership is here to stay, and what all managers (whether straight or gay) need to know about how integrating the G Quotient into their approach to leadership can benefit their career, organization, and employees. At the conclusion of the book, Appendix A offers you an opportunity to take a quick assessment to see how your own beliefs and behaviors about management align with the seven principles of G Quotient leadership.

Because the G Quotient is indeed breaking new ground in the study of business leadership, I would be remiss not to comment on the existence of certain societal obstacles that will no doubt prevent some people from finding the freedom to learn from gay executives. Primarily born out of conservative politics or religious ideology, these obstacles represent beliefs and behaviors that no longer have relevance in the new world of work. As a university educator who has moderated many charged classroom discussions, I guarantee that strong emotions can also make for great dialogue. When accompanied by open minds, such dialogue can serve to enlighten all parties involved.

The following companies and organizations, in whole or within specific working units, have managers identified as G Quotient leaders who participated in my research and are featured throughout the book.

A.T. Kearney	State of Massachusetts
Bain & Company	Mitchell Gold +
Barclay's Bank	Bob Williams
Citicorp	Morgan Stanley
Deloitte Consulting LLP	PepsiCo
Disney	Quest Diagnostics
Ernst & Young	Replacements, Inc.
General Electric	University of California
Hampshire College	University of Southern
IBM	California

To my parents, Edwin and Lula Snyder

Introduction

What Is the G Quotient?

Recently, a colleague I've known and respected for many years called to find out more about "this G Quotient leadership thing" he heard buzzing about the university. I imagine he was expecting some lengthy scholarly discourse, but in the interest of nondisclosure and a terrier that desperately needed walking, I simply said, "It's all about Baskin-Robbins and peanut butter and chocolate ice cream!"

Now if you've ever had this wonderful concoction, I'm sure you'll agree that it's those delicious chunks of peanut butter that compels even the most steadfast dieter to order a triple scoop. As a business case, it's a great lesson in adaptability. Based on highly classified inside information (a high school buddy of mine worked at Baskin Robbins), I was told that the original plan actually called for smooth swirls of peanut butter. However, when the product developers opened the very first batch, they discovered something completely unanticipated (those delicious chunks of peanut butter) and decided to run with it. It was much like my own research process, which led me to the identification of what my normally more eloquent colleague termed, "this G Quotient leadership thing."

My particular field of expertise, which is essentially examining the role of work in contemporary society, offers two general research paths to follow—one of correlation and one of experimentation. While experimentation can lead to great discoveries, I'm not particularly fond of repetition, nor am I patient enough to ever become a true pioneer. As I mentioned in the Preface, my particular aptitude is connecting the dots, and that is exactly how the G Quotient came to life.

The goal of correlational research is to identify a relationship between variables. In the case of this book, it's the correlation between the leadership behaviors of gay male executives and the significantly higher-than-average levels of engagement, job satisfaction, and workplace morale among their employees. From 2000 through 2003, while conducting one of the largest-ever research projects chronicling the career experiences of professional gays and lesbians (which eventually led to my first book, *Lavender Road to Success*), I kept hearing anecdotes that suggested a high level of satisfaction among their employees. Since my focus was on the career experiences of these professionals and not on their employees, I simply noted it as an interesting aside.

During this same period it was clear that the state of the workplace was facing a very real and troubling problem. Among peers in my own field, it was a topic that was heating up all over the country. Word from the front lines of most major business sectors—reflected on the assorted e-mail discussion lists I subscribed to—indicated that indeed employees were growing extremely unhappy with their workplace leadership. One day in particular I recall receiving at least a dozen e-mail messages, some linking me to new articles on the subject and others that were more personal. Friends, colleagues, and readers were also talking to me about how disengaged they were at work. Why? The answers were invariably the same. "My boss doesn't value me" or "I'm tired of feeling like I don't have a voice at work." We've all had our share of bad bosses who manage out of anger or insecurity, but it appeared that this widespread employee unrest was reaching what seemed like epidemic proportions. The needs and expectations of contemporary employees had clearly changed, but the leadership style of most managers did not address or recognize these changes, much less allow for an understanding of the transformation itself.

When I finished my first book, a new research project was waiting in the wings, one that on the surface seemed to be a completely separate endeavor. At the time, I had no idea that I was about to find my own version of peanut-butter-and-chocolate ice cream. My research observations indicated that we had indeed entered a new time in the world of work. The overall expectations and values of today's employees had been completely redefined since the mid-1990s. One phase of my research consisted of surveying recruiters and hiring managers primarily from the Fortune 500. A subsequent phase was developed to determine whether or not there was a difference in levels of employee engagement within different sectors. Because technology makes it possible to segment data and run all types of reports to identify various connections, I started to see a difference not based on sector but on personal demographics. One group I had sent this particular survey to was a small group of gay managers who represented various industries around the country. When I contrasted their assessment of the engagement levels among their employees with those of the greater research group, I was surprised to find a very different set of correlations.

It was at this point that those anecdotal reports of happy employees that I had tucked away in my memory bank from my earlier research grew louder. Standing at the proverbial fork in the road, I decided to go down this new path in pursuit of what turned out to be the G Quotient—the result of which you now hold in your hands.

Why Gay Executives Are in the Right Place at the Right Time

Across the centuries, gay men have been documented as leaders in fields that include the arts, philosophy, science, the military, even government and politics. But not until now have they had widespread success as visible business leaders. To understand why gay executives are currently finding great success as business leaders begins with recognizing how gay men have adapted to their surroundings throughout history. For example, psychological literature informs us that even at very early ages, gay men recognize that they are *different*. As a result, they adapt to the realities of their environments in order to feel emotionally and physically safe. Essentially, it's a matter of survival. But there's a big jump from surviving to thriving.

The G Quotient couldn't have existed in any other time period because of the realities of the emotional closet in which gay men needed to hide in order to feel safe. However, over the past fifty years sociocultural events and circumstances have liberated gay men from marginalized status into acceptable mainstream roles within American society. Today, because it's possible to find success out of the closet in virtually all career fields—although certainly not in all geographic locations—gay men are now using their personal identities as professional assets.

According to the Human Rights Campaign, in 2005, 83 percent of companies in the Fortune 500 included sexual orientation as part of their nondiscrimination policies. In fact, the higher a company is toward the top of the list, the more likely it is to have these policies. Forty-nine—or *98 percent*—of the Fortune 50 companies now provide inclusive environments for their gay and lesbian employees.[1] What prompted these companies to include gays and lesbians in their nondiscrimination policies as well as actively seeking to recruit them as employees? Quite simply, it's proving to be good business.

It might be a great premise for a television program on any number of cable networks, but gay executives did not get together one weekend on Fire Island or in West Hollywood and decide to collectively adopt a new approach to organizational leadership. Instead, the predilection for gay men to base their leadership roles on what I have identified in the book as the seven principles of G Quotient leadership evolved over time; it is based on three fundamental (learned) skills that gay men have developed: *adaptability, intuitive communication*, and *creative problem solving*. To a researcher, one of the reasons why the G Quotient is so intriguing is that it demonstrates the power of human beings to adapt and flourish even against what might seem like insurmountable obstacles. Therefore, I believe it's critical to the subject of business leadership to recognize that, independent of one another, gay executives in all types of fields and industries are managing their employees based on these same principles. The G Quotient wasn't planned— it simply evolved.

Why Now?

No one single event has contributed more or less to the development of G Quotient leadership. Rather, multitudes of contributing phenomena occurring over the past fifty-plus years have resulted in the current leadership success of gay executives. Gay executives are quite simply in the right place at the right time, defined by the simultaneous convergence of the following forces:

- The reconstruction of contemporary employees
- The development and refining of the fundamental learned skills of gay men, primarily but not limited to adaptability, intuitive communication, and creative problem solving
- The social, historical, and political context of our time

Within these overlapping contexts, today's business world has unexpectedly become a setting where gay executives are achieving greater success than other demographic populations as effective corporate leaders and entrepreneurs, as measured by their employees. Because gay executives understand what it's like to have their own value as human beings questioned, they are particularly attuned to the needs of today's empowered employees for respect and value. Essentially, gay executives are the first group of leaders in which G Quotient leadership has been identified due in large part to their belief that every employee has tremendous importance as an individual. To fully understand the evolution of the G Quotient and why it's proving so successful as a leadership paradigm in today's workplace, it's necessary to look in detail at the three converging forces that explain why this is happening now.

The Reconstruction of Contemporary Employees

The seemingly infinite production and dissemination of specialized knowledge on a daily basis has transformed the way employees view their organizational leaders. Knowledge once reserved solely for top-level executives is now readily available to the masses with a simple click. As the primary tool behind employee reconstruction, *knowledge* has completely changed the rules for facilitating employee engagement.

Want to find out what people are really saying about your organization's product line?

Click.

Interested in the salaries and benefits being offered to employees at competing companies?

Click.

Maybe you'd like to read more about that pending lawsuit recently filed against the CEO?

Another click.

Beginning in the mid-1990s, employees in all fields and industries gained widespread access to specialized knowledge that allowed them to peek behind the corporate veil. Simply put, the CEO has no clothes. No matter where you fall on the company's food chain, you can easily view the organization and even its highest leaders in their own professional nakedness. Of course, corporate counter-spin is out there too—primarily from those leaders who are under fire themselves for nefarious behavior. But in the newly recalibrated world of work, leaders no longer have the luxury of hiding their own reality.

Evidence of the struggle among this nation's top executives in their quest to be viewed as successful leaders is evident in the dramatic turnover among the ranks of CEOs. In the first quarter of

2005, Challenger, Gray & Christmas reported that 441 CEOs left their jobs in the United States—an increase of 88 percent over the preceding year.[2] Corporate America is experiencing widespread boardroom emergencies not because all chief executives have suddenly become incompetent but because most leaders don't understand what their employees need.

In addition to the acquisition of specialized work-related knowledge, another important factor contributes to the process of employee reconstruction. With as many personal networks as there are employees, the opportunity to immediately share all this once-unattainable knowledge has exploded beyond measurement. When you put these two factors together in the context of the workplace, the resulting sum is unparalleled *employee empowerment*.

Knowledge + Interconnection = Employee Empowerment

In addition to being empowered through this equation, our society is undeniably shifting toward empowerment in general. In fact, the demand for self-improvement products and services is forecast to continue its upward climb during the next decade. Therefore, it's arguable that the impact on the individual need for finding personal value will climb as well. In a February 2004 report titled "Self-Improvement Products and Services," Marketdata reported that between 2000 and 2004, the market for self-improvement products and services increased by a whopping 50 percent. By 2008, Marketdata forecasts that the self-help and self-improvement industry will reach $12 billion, up from $5.7 billion in 2000.

According to Simba Information, widely recognized as a leading authority for market intelligence and forecasts in the media industry, sales from self-help and self-improvement books alone jumped from $611 million in 2000 to $640 million in 2003.[3] Represented by the desire to improve mentally, physically, and financially, the quest for self-improvement is a need that can be said to apply to all types of people representing the gamut of demographic circumstances.

From books to television to cable news, these messages place primary importance on the individual, and therefore make an immeasurable impact on the way employees view their own professional roles. It has arguably contributed to the change in how people view themselves in their role as employees. The need among empowered employees to be valued is proving a successful match with G Quotient leadership—as shown in Appendix D, more than 86 percent of employees reporting to gay managers believe their ideas and opinions *matter*. It's a state of being that has made a significant and positive impact on employee engagement, job satisfaction, and workplace morale in G Quotient environments.

The Learned Skills of Gay Men

The origins of today's high level of visibility and acceptance of gays and lesbians can be traced back to the visionary ideals of social pioneers such as Harry Hay, founder of the Mattachine Society. Secretly meeting in private homes in Los Angeles and other cities across the nation, the members of Mattachine were the forbears of the gay liberation movement, opening the closet doors for the development of the G Quotient. More than fifty years ago, Hay felt that as a community, gay men were unique and had something important to offer humanity in general. Hay spoke of gay men as "spirit people" who, across the centuries, served the greater good through roles that included "messengers and interceders, image-makers and prophets, mimes and rhapsodes, poets and playwrights, healers and nurturers, teachers and preachers, searchers and researchers."[4] Collectively, they represent the historical beginnings of the three fundamental learned skills (adaptability, intuitive communication, and creative problem solving) demonstrated by today's gay executives.

Adaptability. Richard Isay, the first non-closeted gay affirmative psychiatrist of the American Psychoanalytic Association and author of the noteworthy books *Being Homosexual: Gay Men and their Development* and *Becoming Gay: The Journey to Self-Acceptance*, states that being gay typically includes taking on the role of "outsider" within society. In fact, most gay men report that at an early age, even before consciously acknowledging their sexual orientation, they clearly identify themselves as being different from those around them. This recognition typically results in an awareness of a need to adapt their verbal and nonverbal communication in an effort to prevent "displeasure" from caretakers or other influential people in their lives. As a result, they perceive the world differently.

As part of the recognition process of being different, gay men tend to develop an accompanying self-awareness and basic critical thinking in order to get along in the world. Walt Odets, a clinical psychologist in San Francisco, presents this recognition process as a lifelong dynamic rooted in tenacity and strength as gay men forge lives that express who they are as human beings. According to Odets, gay men *have to think* consciously about their feelings, their reactions to others, and their longing for human love and companionship. Over time, these mental processes have contributed to significant levels of personal insight. While Odets notes that gay men are psychologically a lot like straight men, he points out that they have uniquely reinvented themselves in a search for personal empowerment and meaning. In so doing, they have distinguished their own needs from the expectations of society.[5]

Intuitive Communication.   In preparation for coming out, gay men instinctively develop and refine their ability to scan their environment so as to become aware of and predict the emotional responses of others. This requires them to sift through a great deal of information to quickly distinguish what is relevant from what is irrelevant and can therefore be discarded—a skill that has played a particularly strong role in the G Quotient's evolution. In fact, it's directly tied to the ability among G Quotient leaders to use their professional intuition effectively to make successful business decisions ranging from hiring staff to selecting new marketing channels for products and services, detailed further in Chapter Six.

In many respects, this ability can be thought of as an early warning system, or, as psychologists term it, the "adaptive unconscious." The adaptive unconscious is explained exceptionally well in Malcolm Gladwell's *Blink*. In application, this intuitive skill acts as a "content filter" for thoughts and feelings that enables its possessor to pick up on a wide range of often subtle but meaningful verbal and nonverbal communication cues.[6] In using this skill, gay men have become particularly adept at quickly sizing up their environment using "rapid cognition" or flashes of insight to facilitate both their survival and their safety. While certainly a subjective experience, it nonetheless enables gay executives to respond professionally to their own internal voice or intuition in order to identify what can simply be termed as *friend* or *foe*, *organizational ally* or *adversary*.

In terms of intuitive communication skills, the universal experience of coming out requires exacting insight to examine not only one's basic feelings, but one's assumptions and emotional attachments at a highly authentic level. When successfully navigated, this process results in a reinvention of one's very identity—somewhat analogous to the reconstruction of employees that has occurred over the last decade. Therefore, among the gay executives identified as G Quotient leaders, there is more than an awareness of the value of transformation, there is also an *appreciation* for its usefulness.

Creative Problem Solving. While traveling through Chicago's O'Hare Airport on my way to a conference, carry-on luggage in hand, I noticed that according to the departure boards my connecting flight was in another terminal. Now if you've ever traveled through O'Hare, you know that automatic sidewalks link the terminals together to transport passengers methodically and safely throughout the airport. On this particular day, the automatic sidewalks seemed to be moving very slowly. Since I had limited time to make my connecting flight, I decided to take my chances in the pedestrian aisle adjacent to the airport "people mover." As I began my journey, I couldn't help but notice how the people on the automatic sidewalks were so at ease—they were talking on cell phones, chatting, some were even reading books and newspapers. Basically, they exerted little effort as they moved forward toward their shared destination. For me and everyone else walking in the pedestrian aisle, we didn't have that same luxury. We had to continually dodge oncoming traffic, detour around new floor installations, and when walking behind someone traveling too slow, overtake and pass. In other words, our view of the world and our experience in it was very different from that of the passengers on the automatic sidewalks.

Because the conference I was headed to was about workplace equality for gays and lesbians, I was also thinking about my presentation. Suddenly it occurred to me that as a metaphor for traditional society, straight people are on automatic sidewalks. Over the course of their lives, straight people are taken through a proven and safe path that typically includes dating, the prom, getting married, having children, grandchildren, and so onward to the end. Whatever their very real troubles may be, they haven't much need to worry about societal or environmental obstacles getting in their way because their course, and therefore their worldview, is for the most part consistent and clear. Gay executives are not on automatic sidewalks. They are in the pedestrian aisle. As a result of this experience, their worldview (often developed against traffic and in the face of a variety of societal and environmental obstacles) is quite different. Without automatic sidewalks, it's necessary to learn creative ways to navigate your path to reach your destination safely. In terms of G Quotient leadership, it's this very experience that has contributed to the leadership belief system of gay executives that is being successfully applied in workplaces in the four defined business sectors—Fortune 500 companies, government, colleges and universities, and small business—that I have studied.

From Surviving to Thriving

While conducting research for this book, I was struck by the strong parallels between the acceptance of women and the acceptance of gay men as business leaders. I found these parallels to be much more than just a loose thread connecting the last three decades. The historical obstacles faced by all women in the pursuit of success as business leaders strongly resemble those that many gay men face today. Most noteworthy is the correlation between the Equal Rights Amendment (ERA) and the Employment Non-Discrimination Act (ENDA). Even though the ERA was approved by Congress in 1972, it still failed to achieve formal ratification by the states, mainly due to societal influences related to regional beliefs, conservative politics, and religious ideology. These are the same influences that ultimately killed ENDA, the gay and lesbian equivalent of the Equal Rights Amendment.

While societal influences deal with external forces, a more internal parallel connects women and gay men, and it speaks to the very definition of G Quotient leadership. It's about doing business in a different way. In fact, it's about being in the world in a different way. Thirty years ago, most management types (primarily straight white males) didn't think there was anything to be learned from women in business—mostly as a result of the previously mentioned societal influences. And while women still face significant gender bias in today's workplace, they are achieving as successful CEOs, senators, governors, and university presidents. It is estimated that they will soon outnumber men as entrepreneurs.[7]

I found that among the gay executives interviewed for this book, many had been helped along early in their careers by women. In fact, one executive said, "As a gay man, I have had some of my best professional experiences under the management of women. When working closely together, there's an effective balance and camaraderie that can be achieved between masculine and feminine ideals because there isn't the threat of sexual involvement or related tensions. There's also a greater sense of 'out with the old and in with the new' that can lead to all types of new discoveries and successes." But despite the many parallels between the quest for business success between women and gay men, there are also distinct differences. Most prominently in my opinion is the fact that while gender is accepted as being a product of biological factors, sexual orientation has, until recently, been viewed as a lifestyle or choice.

Scientific studies over the past two decades, and specifically in the twenty-first century, have confirmed a number of physiological connections that I believe play a role in explaining why all this is happening now. Using sophisticated medical imaging techniques, scientists have identified definite genetic components and brain structures related to the determinant of sexual identity as being primarily biological. Likewise, the development of gay affirmative psychology and self-improvement books, which emerged during this same period, took a substantially different viewpoint from earlier psychological theories, which held that gay men needed to be "cured." At its very heart, gay affirmative psychology takes the approach that there is nothing inherently wrong with individuals who identify as gay and lesbian. Instead of succumbing to the oppressive social construct of the closet, most gay men understand that suppressing their sexual orientation in an attempt to take on what society has viewed as the more socially acceptable role of heterosexuality can lead to a variety of emotional stresses and difficulties, including diminished career health.

The Social, Historical, and Political Contexts of G Quotient Leadership

Because *The G Quotient* isn't a book about gay history, the time line presented here is merely an overview of the social and political events that have contributed to the development of G Quotient leadership. It certainly isn't representative of the entire scope of the gay and lesbian movement, but it's enough to present the historical events and cultural milieu that explains, in part, why gay executives are in the right place at the right time.

William Naphy, in his expansive 2004 cross-cultural review, *Born to Be Gay: A History of Homosexuality*, documents how being gay has always been a societal force. It's just that until now, it hasn't been documented as a *business* force. In identifying the long sweep of historical attitudes and sociocultural constructions of sex and sexuality in general, Naphy found that, ultimately, sexual orientation is merely a very real characteristic of the human species. In other words, when taken as part of the greater human condition, being gay is simply a part of the human sexuality continuum.

Throughout history, being gay has been accepted with varying degrees of approval or disapproval in various cultures at various times. In fact, the evolution and existence of the G Quotient as a leadership paradigm exemplifies this point. Louis Crompton, in his 2003 sociological world review, *Homosexuality and Civilization*, states that "the history of civilization reveals, above all, how differently homosexuality has been perceived and judged at different times in different cultures" (p. xiii). Crompton documents that among the ancient Greeks, for example, being gay was associated with courage in battle, philosophical mentorship, and the defense of democracy. In China, same-sex love and devotion included the loves of emperors, Fujian "marriages," and Mandarin scholars paired with opera stars. In Japan, same-sex romantic relationships, or *nanshoku* (male love) was associated with Buddhist saints, samurai warriors, and the kabuki theater (pp. xiii-xiv).

James E. Van Buskirk, a reviewer for *Library Journal*, discussing Martin Duberman's *Hidden from History: Reclaiming the Gay and Lesbian Past* (1990), eloquently summed it up this way: "Being gay is not merely a personal characteristic to be alternatively ignored or celebrated, as some historians have assumed, but a significant influence on the lives of individuals and on patterns of cultural organizations in ways historians need to acknowledge."[8]

When Alfred C. Kinsey published his landmark book, *Sexual Behavior in the Human Male*, in 1948, he argued that sexual expression was a continuum and the notions of sexual activity being conveniently labeled "normal" and "abnormal" were inaccurate and unproductive. Instead, Kinsey replaced these terms with "common" and "uncommon." Most notably, his work shocked the American public with its finding that some 37 percent of (white) men in the United States had engaged in sex with another male at some time in their lives. Kinsey's work was underscored in 1951 with the work of Cleland Ford and Frank Beach, who analyzed more than seventy cultures outside the United States in *Patterns of Sexual Behavior*. They found that in those cultures for which such information was available, forty-nine overtly sanctioned homosexual behavior as "normal."

Following in Kinsey's footsteps, psychologist Evelyn Hooker did a great service to scientific inquiry with her 1957 publication, *The Adjustment of the Male Overt Homosexual*. Noted for her scientific objectivity, Hooker used standard psychological tests to disprove the claims of those who said that homosexuals were diseased and psychologically damaged. She wrote, "What is difficult to accept (for most clinicians) is that some homosexuals may be very ordinary individuals, indistinguishable from ordinary individuals who are heterosexual."[9] In large part due to Kinsey and Hooker, laws regulating private sexual relations between consenting adults were dropped on the recommendation of the American Bar Association in 1961. Together, Kinsey and Hooker set the stage for the sexual liberation social movement that would define the next two decades and become a factor in the evolution of G Quotient leadership.

The gay movement then began to gain momentum in the 1960s following the development of the black civil rights movement, the women's movement, and the antiwar movement. In a social context, all these movements were about questioning long-held assumptions about basic civil rights. It became acceptable and even valuable to publicly question authority—analogous to what today's workers are experiencing as a result of employee empowerment. Collectively, these movements "challenged America's preconceptions . . . and shook up its categories of what's right, wrong, normal and abnormal" just as Kinsey and Hooker had done in the preceding decade.[10] Millions of Americans were freed from the commonly held belief that sex should be viewed solely for procreation.

In 1969, the events at Stonewall Inn in New York City, widely considered to be the actual day when the gay movement officially began, became a lightning rod for recognizing the need to change the way society addresses its gay and lesbian citizens. Refusing to be intimidated by police force and gratuitous harassment, participants in the Stonewall riots brought heightened visibility to the gay community. In 1970, immediately on the heels of Stonewall, the National Association for Mental Health declared that homosexuality between consenting adults should be decriminalized. The American Psychiatric Association then followed suit in 1973 and struck homosexuality from its *Diagnostic Manual of Psychiatric Disorders*. Two years later in 1975, the American Psychological Association did the same. It was, in effect, emancipation.

Over the course of time between the 1960s and mid-1980s, the advancement of gay rights as well as the role gays and lesbians openly played in society was akin to stepping out of the Dark Ages for several generations of citizens. All over the country, gay pride events and social awareness increased as the grip of oppression slowly began to ease.[11] Then in the mid-1980s things changed again. In developing this Introduction, I often found myself wondering if the G Quotient would exist if the AIDS crisis had not hit the gay community, temporarily slowing the momentum toward equal rights while forcing community members to develop business and social solutions to this unparalleled catastrophe. Both play a role in today's simultaneous convergence of the three forces outlined earlier in this Introduction.

Seemingly overnight, community-based organizations were formed to provide services, comfort, and solutions. Gay men learned from lesbians, already well-versed in feminist politics, that the power of health care was directly related to the power of one's position in society. Building on the ideals of the public health centers of the 1970s as well as many of the groups and organizations that were formed during this same period, gay men acquired newfound empowerment through both economic and social activism. Collectively and individually they rallied, becoming politically savvy, economically active, and socially powerful.

Yet along with this positive shift toward empowerment came enormous multiple losses and recurring bereavement. In the midst of their overwhelming loss and grief, gay men as a community sharpened their organizational abilities while refusing to return to lives of secrecy, prejudice, and isolation. From an evolutionary perspective, these experiences further contributed to the development of the three fundamental skills associated with gay executives: *adaptability, intuitive communication*, and *creative problem solving*. The 1990s witnessed the open policy of the Clinton administration (the first presidential campaign to recognize and include gay voters), non-closeted gay elected officials, and the highly publicized television coming-out of Ellen Degeneres. This was followed later in the decade by what seemed outrageous at the time, *Will and Grace*. Consider where we are today. Ellen's coming out is now considered old hat, *Queer as Folk* successfully pushed the envelope for six years on cable, *Will and Grace* no longer shocks as it ends its award-winning seven-year run, *Queer Eye for the Straight Guy* unapologetically comes into the homes of millions of Americans, and Ang Lee's *Brokeback Mountain* won top honors all over the world. In this new century, the issue of gay marriage—whether you agree with it or not, and even during a conservative presidential administration—is gaining acceptance and remains on the table of public discussion. Never before would it have been possible for gay executives to succeed as business leaders in organizations all across the country, from large metropolitan cities to smaller and even rural settings. Beginning with Kinsey almost sixty years ago and continuing through to the amazing success of *Brokeback Mountain*, all the social and political events that happened in between contributed to the evolution of the G Quotient and explain why, in today's recalibrated world of work, gay executives are indeed in the right place at the right time.

The Seven Principles of G Quotient Leadership

The G Quotient is an emerging paradigm for successful leadership based on seven specific management principles. As the tangible expressions of what defines G Quotient leadership, I believe, each of the seven principles needs a clear definition. The seven principles provide context and meaning to all of the concepts presented throughout this book, and play a central role in explaining why gay executives are the first group of managers to be identified as practitioners of this new leadership paradigm. I invite you to refer back to this list often as a point of reference as you move forward in *The G Quotient*.

Principle One: Inclusion

Inclusion is viewed as the fundamental source of organizational success in G Quotient environments. Gay executives inspire their employees to become engaged in their work and committed to excellence through a demonstrated respect for the individual value of each employee. As shown in Appendix D, in these settings, employee motivation stems from leadership that inspires rather than rules, with 84 percent of employees reporting that they are always treated fairly by their manager.

Employees describe their gay managers as motivators rather than dictators, and my research found that, as a principle of leadership, inclusion is much more about acts and behavior than language and organizational policies. In G Quotient environments, gay executives frequently convey respect and value for their employees through a variety of employee-centered programs and benefits. Believing that investing in the value of their employees' lives is not just the right thing to do but also advantageous to their organizations, gay executives use their collective and deeply held convictions about equality to successfully drive all the processes of work within their own organizations.

Principle Two: Creativity

In G Quotient environments, creativity is considered a primary source of forward organizational movement, centered on three focus points identified as *concepts*, *possibilities*, and *people*. My research found that gay executives typically define creativity as the ability to look at ideas in fresh new ways and define innovation as the economic by-product it yields. In this context, creativity is acknowledged as an employee process and innovation as an organizational product. Creativity is also a professional goal for employees within these environments across all four business sectors. Among employees reporting to gay managers, 85 percent reported that people with different ideas are valued in their workplace environment. Comparatively, the 2005 Towers Perrin study mentioned earlier found that only 41 percent of employees think their senior management supports new ideas and new ways of doing things.

Connecting these three focus points together has become a proven route to innovation within these environments. Other organizational benefits associated with creativity as a principle of G Quotient leadership include enhanced problem-solving capabilities and more effective bridges with organizational stakeholders, as well as higher employee retention and increased workplace morale.

Principle Three: Adaptability

As the third principle of G Quotient leadership, adaptability addresses the willingness and capacity to adapt to change, particularly in the greater economic, social, and political landscapes of the world. My research found that gay executives believe their organizations must develop an awareness and appreciation for the concept of change or face difficulty in developing and building new strategies to remain competitive. In G Quotient environments, being able to adapt to the concept of change has guarded against organizational groupthink and contributed to significantly higher levels of employee engagement and commitment to excellence.

In these organizations, the ambiguity that often accompanies change is considered an acceptable state of professional being. Ambiguity or "living with gray" is viewed as a necessary component of forward organizational movement. In this context, gay executives and their employees regularly respond to new opportunities with a state of professional readiness, accepting that it may be necessary to move quickly in a new direction as appropriate for the particular situation or event.

Principle Four: Connectivity

Connectivity is considered to represent the functional network on which G Quotient environments are assembled, supported and advanced. As a principle of leadership, connectivity follows adaptability because change mandates a subsequent need to acquire new perspectives and professional tools in order to maximize organizational success. In G Quotient environments, connectivity takes on two forms: external networking and internal awareness. And in G Quotient environments, connectivity is viewed to be the mechanism that keeps gay executives and their employees in touch with both organizational and industry movement, providing a competitive edge.

Employees in G Quotient environments report less professional isolation, enhanced job performance, and significantly higher levels of workplace happiness and contentment. My research found that gay executives believe their organizations must continually draw from outside sources of knowledge to reach their full potential.

Principle Five: Communication

G Quotient environments are based on a foundation of authenticity and trust. As a principle of leadership, communication as an open system actively develops and nurtures interaction in order to create a culture that encourages and supports trust, facilitates organizational candor, and promotes cohesiveness. My research found that authenticity actually provides gay executives with the type of internal credibility that ultimately allows them to promote communication with their employees, using the strength of their own individuality.

In these settings, gay executives consistently and freely share information with their employees about the course and direction of the organization. As a result, employees report, this extremely high level of professional disclosure contributes to greater trust within the workplace environment. Among employees reporting to gay managers, 90 percent reported that information and knowledge are shared openly in their environment. Nationally, the Challenger, Gray & Christmas Report notes, only 36 percent of employees think senior management communicates the reasons for important business decisions effectively.

Principle Six: Intuition

Intuition as a principle of G Quotient leadership is about gut instinct based on perceived truth. In G Quotient environments, intuition plays a positive role in decision making on issues ranging from personnel matters to developing new business relationships to committing to new deals and projects. Gay executives view intuition as a business asset and encourage their employees to develop and apply their own set of professional instincts.

In G Quotient environments, integrating intuition into the decision-making process has resulted in better hires, greater utilization of employee talent, and increased workplace harmony because people are assembled into teams that complement individual strengths. Gay executives typically use their ability to collect information through indirect as opposed to direct sources, enabling them to effect greater reasoning and processing of all types of business information in their organizations.

Principle Seven: Collaboration

In G Quotient environments, collaboration contributes to employee engagement and job satisfaction because it contributes to the equilibrium of the organization as a whole. Gay executives build cultures where collaboration enhances all the conceptual and physical processes associated with organizational development and management. My research found that this type of collaboration lessens "me first" antagonism, which often takes over in those settings where everyone feels that their own success must come at the failure (or diminished success) of others. In this context, gay executives use collaboration to create environments that are more welcoming, affirming, and balanced.

As the final principle of G Quotient leadership, collaboration depends upon and grows out of the practice of each of the other six. Without inclusion, creativity, adaptability, connectivity, communication, and intuition, *collaboration* will always struggle for existence because in order to be effective, an organization requires a new ethos of leadership that fully takes advantage of the potential of today's empowered employees.

A New Quotient for a New Age

The G Quotient is not an intelligence quotient (IQ), nor is it emotional intelligence (EQ). While IQ and EQ encompass potentially infinite influences, "GQ" is derived from a finite set of seven influences—identified in this book as leadership principles. An IQ is traditionally considered to be a reflection of an individual's cognitive capacity in comparison to the general population. It's a measure of ability to understand concepts and solve problems. EQ on the other hand, as it implies, is about *emotions*. First defined by professors Peter Salovey of Yale University and John Mayer of the University of New Hampshire in 1990, it is (in its originators' phrase) "an ability to recognize the meanings of emotion and their relationships, and to reason and problem-solve on the basis of them."[12]

Uniquely relevant to the workplace, GQ measures one's propensity toward G Quotient leadership based on the seven identified leadership principles. The purpose of this measurement is to gain a better understanding about one's own approach to leadership in the context of today's workplace. As noted, Appendix A offers an opportunity to take the new GQ assessment at the end of this book.

The G Quotient reflects the leveling of knowledge in work-places where employees no longer view themselves as "less than." A step beyond understanding one's emotions and the ramifications of those emotions, G Quotient leadership actually unites employees and their managers through practical and meaningful connections based on a communication platform of equality. Moving into the first section of the book, I believe it's important to consider that the significant success of G Quotient leadership signals what is likely the final shift in the need for management to focus on the processes of work rather than the final product—180 degrees opposite the focus of leadership paradigms still rooted in Industrial Age principles.

Part One

THE SEVEN PRINCIPLES OF G QUOTIENT LEADERSHIP

The G Quotient is about leaders who are making a positive impact on the world of work—and, more specifically, on those who inhabit it. To fully communicate the effectiveness of G Quotient leadership, I knew from the beginning, it would require taking the research findings beyond facts and figures and making them come to life. While the Introduction of this book focuses on how G Quotient leadership among gay executives evolved and why it's making a positive difference in the recalibrated workplace, Part One focuses on its functional and emotional core.

In practice, I found that the seven identified principles of G Quotient leadership unquestionably explain why so many employees under the direct management of gay executives are more engaged, more satisfied in their jobs, and report greater levels of workplace morale than employees in other types of environments. *Why are gay executives winning the leadership race?* The insights, perspectives, and experiences of the gay executives profiled over the next seven chapters answer that question. Some are making their impact in high-profile positions, while others are making an equal impact in roles that don't necessarily generate newspaper headlines or magazine articles. What I believe this demonstrates is that the effectiveness of G Quotient leadership is just as great for executives who manage organizations with ten employees as it is for those who manage organizations with a thousand employees.

1

PRINCIPLE ONE: INCLUSION

Across all four business sectors I researched (Fortune 500 companies, government, colleges and universities, and small business), gay executives overwhelmingly believe that their commitment to inclusion is a fundamental source of their leadership success. Regardless of the field or industry, my research identified inclusion as the overarching principle that guides gay executives in inspiring their employees to become fully engaged in their work and committed to excellence as *equal participants* in the organization. This first principle of inclusion is what tethers the G Quotient to its own framework of efficacy. Because G Quotient leadership is built upon complementary beliefs and principles, without inclusion as its guiding credo, the other six principles would have little if any meaning or impact.

While G Quotient environments typically consist of employees who reflect diverse demographic backgrounds, I found that as a principle of leadership, inclusion is less about diversity and much more about equality. Because inclusion and diversity are often used interchangeably, it's important to distinguish between the two so as to provide a clear understanding about how this first principle makes a positive impact in these environments.

Consider that diversity focuses on *differences*—different cultures, ages, and sexual orientations. Inclusiveness focuses on sameness. In this context, *sameness* means that all employees are given equal support to succeed in the organization based on their manager's demonstrated commitment to individual value. Because

> *Eighty-two percent of gay executives report that they always believe that diverse populations result in diverse talents and skills, all of which they affirm are necessary for the success of their organizations.*

G Quotient environments represent true meritocracies, employees will or will not succeed based solely on their individual abilities and initiative.

For gay executives and their employees, I found inclusion to be defined much more by acts and behaviors than by language and organizational policies. In the words of one Fortune 500 employee, "Lip service doesn't count anymore." Consistently described by their employees as *motivators* rather than *dictators*, G Quotient leaders frequently convey respect and value for their employees in two ways—through *economic tangibles* and *emotional tangibles*. Economic tangibles refer to those employee-centered benefits and programs that require some type of financial investment by the company, regardless of whether its purpose is to enhance life external to or internal to the workplace. Emotional tangibles, on the other hand, equally convey respect and value, but deal with more personal commodities such as confidence and trust. As a fundamental part of their own makeup, inclusion can be considered second nature for the majority of gay executives profiled in this book for the reasons described earlier. It's about that different worldview gay executives develop from walking down the pedestrian aisle instead of being on the automatic sidewalks.

Building an Inclusive Empire:
Mitchell Gold and Bob Williams
Founders, Mitchell Gold + Bob Williams

Mitchell Gold and Bob Williams have built a furniture empire based on respect for their employees, customers, and business partners. Since 1989, when they created The Mitchell Gold Company, renamed in 2005 as Mitchell Gold + Bob Williams, these award-winning entrepreneurs have revolutionized their industry in design and corporate leadership. To a great extent, their success story is the result of the positive relationship they've consciously created between three organizational ingredients: vision for the company, products and services, and approach to leadership.

While some companies can become successful based on two of these three ingredients—never just one—it's rare to sustain and grow that success without the ability to manage and capitalize on all three. Beginning with their vision for manufacturing furniture based on trends they first observed in the apparel industry, their products quickly became synonymous with style, quality, comfort, and service. At the same time, the company itself became known as one of the best and most inclusive places to work in the entire country.

In companies where gay executives are also founding officers, this first principle of inclusion has, without question, shaded all aspects of organizational development from the very beginning. Without the constraints of preexisting corporate structures, as in the case of Mitchell Gold + Bob Williams, G Quotient leaders are free to build organizational cultures from the ground up—based entirely on their own set of beliefs and principles.

As already described, the likelihood that gay executives will place a greater emphasis on the individual value of their employees is connected to their experience of being in society in a different way. Mitchell and Bob told me that one of their biggest motivators for creating a company where respect and value are unwavering ideals is the discrimination they have experienced in their own lives. "In a practical sense," they said, "it's actually one of the benefits of being gay; you learn to respect the fact that all human beings are important, and that's always been a driving force behind the success of our company."

Their belief that "all human beings are important" is most telling in relationship to the location of their company's headquarters in Taylorsville, North Carolina. A conservative region not known for being gay-friendly, this is decidedly a long way from New York,

Los Angeles, or San Francisco. The reason I believe this is so significant is that their commitment to respect and value in the workplace, and their related approach to organizational leadership, has transcended the seemingly entrenched social barriers typically associated with the region's conservative, fundamentalist ideologies. Today, the company is one of the most sought-after employers among straight people in the region.

Inclusion as a leadership principle centers on the need to promote equality in the workplace that isn't just about perceived minority communities or personal affiliations. On this subject, Mitchell and Bob were the first to bring up how strongly they believe in the importance that straight employees never feel "less valuable" than gay employees. It's an interesting point that I heard repeatedly from other gay executives as well. In fact, many of the smaller workplace environments had no gay employees at all.

Having worked with many of the nation's top employers over the last decade, I can attest to the fact that finding organizations that are diverse but not inclusive is unfortunately an easy task. On the other hand, inclusive organizations are typically always diverse because they value the strength of individual difference. I've also found that in non-inclusive environments, employee diversity often creates a sizable barrier to organizational movement rather than acting as a propellant. Why? Because if diversity is to benefit an organization, *inclusion* must be part of the culture in order to prevent the homogeny of talents, skills, and ideas.

> Much of our leadership success is the direct result of our ability to look at people as unique individuals. From a management perspective, one of our core beliefs has always been that every employee should be treated with dignity and respect. Employee motivation begins with creating an environment where everyone has a place of importance.
>
> —Mitchell Gold and Bob Williams

As entrepreneurs and organizational leaders, Mitchell and Bob live a commitment to inclusion that has proven extremely successful.

From the beginning, we have always believed that good leadership goes beyond just talking about doing the right thing. If you don't back your words up with action, you lose credibility. As a company, we have consistently demonstrated our commitment to equality and fair play by taking on the responsibility to improve the quality of life for our employees and their families, in addition to making the working environment as hospitable and enjoyable as possible. For us, it's about respecting the fact that all human beings are important—that's what real family values are all about.

—Mitchell Gold and Bob Williams

They have more than seven hundred employees, and their furniture is sold in the stores of top home retailers, including Pottery Barn, Crate & Barrel, and Restoration Hardware. In addition, almost twenty showrooms across the nation bear their own name. Even with all the press and accolades, their factory in Taylorsville, often referred to as the furniture capital of the United States, remains the heart and soul of their company. It's also where Mitchell and Bob "walk the talk" of respect and value on a daily basis.

Beyond the benefits designed to improve the general quality of life for their workforce, including a scholarship program for employees and their children, annual health fairs, and an on-site day care and child enrichment center, I found a commitment to improving life *inside* the workplace as well. In North Carolina, where humid summer temperatures often reach 100 degrees, Mitchell Gold + Bob Williams was the first company in the area to provide its employees with an air-conditioned factory. One of the more unusual inside improvements that also contributes to a greater level of work-life balance is something they call the "Comfort Zone." The Comfort Zone is a dedicated space in the factory where employees can take advantage of a variety of concierge services, ranging from dry cleaning to car washing.

Targeting a more basic level of human need—food and facilities—the company provides an on-site café for employees with not just a cook but a *chef*. As for the facilities, the bathrooms are cleaned twice a day to provide a better standard of living in the working environment itself.

Collectively, these employee-centered benefits and programs unquestionably play a pivotal role in explaining why the company has the lowest rate of employee turnover in Alexander County as well as industry-high levels of productivity. Mitchell Gold + Bob Williams is a company that has done more than change an industry, as Chapter Ten describes, it has also changed the worldview of its employees.

Why Inclusion Paves the Way for Motivation

It's impossible to talk about inclusion without talking about *motivation*. Inspiring employees to become more engaged in their jobs and committed to excellence depends on the presence of corresponding positive levels of personal motivation. As an employee-centered paradigm rather than a management-centered one, G Quotient leadership ties personal motivation to the leadership principle of inclusion. Think of leadership that *inspires* rather than *rules*. To inspire empowered employees to become engaged in their work, leaders must first commit to the development of an organization that affirms the value of its workforce. In practice, it represents how fair treatment is ultimately facilitated in these environments.

Everyone can agree that, from the Industrial Age to the Digital Age, one of management's primary goals has been to accomplish organizational objectives through employee motivation. Going back more than ninety years, Henry Ford recognized this business truth in 1914 when he paid employees $5 a day, which at the time was approximately twice the salary other manufacturers were paying. How did this affect Ford's employees? Ford Motor Company

> *Over 90 percent of gay executives reported that justice and equity is always a basic rule of their approach to leadership.*

became one of the giants of the Industrial Age due in large part to the commitment of its employees during that era. Ford also recognized that by paying his employees more money, he made it possible for them to afford the very products they manufactured, which further contributed to motivation and engagement issues. Basically, it facilitated pride of workmanship because they were consumers as well as producers.[1]

While salary is certainly a prime source of worker motivation, the reconstruction of contemporary employees has created a new context for this issue. Today, empowered employees primarily view fair and equitable salaries foremost as a demonstration of respect and value rather than as the dollars and cents they need for survival. In this context, the issue of salary is less about purchasing power and more about how it meets the emotional needs of empowered employees. Indeed, according to a 2005 Hudson survey of ten thousand U.S. workers, when asked what job-related factors were most likely to cause them to look for a new job, salary dollars took a deferential backseat to career development and the quality of the manager-employee relationship—both prominent elements of G Quotient leadership.[2]

Without motivation among its people, an organization's struggle to be forward moving often deteriorates into a workplace tug-of-war between managers and employees that wastes everyone's time. Particularly when it comes to job engagement, empowered employees cannot be *ordered* into action effectively. Managers who try to dictate employee engagement in the recalibrated workplace simply succeed in galvanizing their workforce in opposition to whatever they say or do. On one end of the rope you'll see managers flexing their chain-of-command muscles in an attempt to pull employees into action. On the other end, employees dig in their heels as they try to pull management to the ground.

In contrast, tug-of-war matches rarely take place in G Quotient environments because the principle of inclusion overshadows most types of disagreements that arise out of hierarchal separation. But rather than blurring the demarcation line between managers and employees, inclusion transforms "us against them" into a positive unification of both sides. In G Quotient environments, managers and employees are more likely to view each other as being on the same side, working together in a collective effort toward shared organizational goals.

David McClelland (1917–1998), widely recognized in both academic and business circles as the foremost authority in achievement-based motivation, described three types of motivational needs found in the majority of all employees and managers. McClelland, after earning his doctorate in psychology at Yale, pioneered the concept of *workplace motivational thinking* as a professor and researcher at Wesleyan, Harvard, and Boston University. Focusing on personality and consciousness, McClelland asserted that most people display some combination of the following three types of workplace motivation:[3]

- *Achievement motivation:* People motivated by achievement are characterized by an individual need to succeed. They seek to advance in their organizational role while attaining realistic yet challenging goals.

- *Authority and power motivation:* People motivated by power and authority have a need to be influential and effective, making a strong impact on their respective organizations as they seek to increase their own personal status and prestige.

- *Affiliation motivation:* People motivated by the need for friendly and collegial interaction with others also have the desire to be liked. They are typically team players in the workplace.

I found that the majority of gay executives identified in my research are motivated by all three of McClelland's identified types, in varying degrees, accompanied with the belief that each is socially and morally acceptable. In this sense, whether motivation is derived from the need to achieve, the desire for authority and power, or the need to be liked, it is widely viewed by these gay executives as respectable.

Whether or not the integration of all three of McClelland's motivational types into one group of individuals can be considered statistically remarkable is an arguable point. However, what is remarkable is that there's a definite mirroring of how employees in these same settings define their own workplace motivation. That is, G Quotient leadership creates environments that encourage employees to find motivation through these same influences. When the collective environment shares similar definitions of their professional needs and wants, the organization or working unit becomes more integrated, focused, and productive.

Motivating Through Inclusion:
Greg Morley
Director, Disney

As HR director for Hong Kong Disneyland and a member of the Hong Kong Disneyland Taskforce, Greg Morley is an international leader at Disney. Beginning his career with the company in 1995 at Epcot in Orlando, Florida, he quickly began his ascent through the ranks in the entertainment giant.

After repeated promotions in Orlando, which took him from Epcot at Walt Disney World to Disney Cruise Line, Greg was offered the position of director of recruitment at Disneyland in Southern California, during its transformation into Disneyland Resort in 2000. In one of the company's most visible HR positions, he had the responsibility of hiring more than nine thousand employees during the expansion process. The following year he was asked to lead Disney University at Disneyland Resort Paris, a resounding testament to his success. After two subsequent promotions in Paris, where he ultimately led organizational change efforts during a time of significant transformation, Greg was recruited to Hong Kong, where Disney was preparing to open its newest theme park, Hong Kong Disneyland. Greg came on board before the park's grand opening, and he was able to call on his earlier success in Southern California, building a human resources team to support five thousand new cast members at Hong Kong Disneyland. Throughout each of these roles and across many different continents, his belief in inclusion has been a centerpiece of his leadership.

On the day of our scheduled interview, Greg e-mailed me from the train on his morning commute. It was already the next day in Hong Kong, and I felt like I was getting a jumpstart on my own next workday. One of the first topics we discussed was something Greg has become an expert at in three very disparate cultures—how to

> Team dynamics driven by culture and context may be different in France versus China or even between the U.S. East and West Coast. Fundamentally, human beings want to be appreciated, valued, and have the opportunity to learn. One of the reasons I believe I've been successful across several different cultures is because I'm able to appreciate human differences as valuable.
>
> —Greg Morley

hire and motivate thousands of employees in a very short time. To get everyone on the same page and moving toward the same organizational goals, Greg believes, the leadership principle of inclusion must be the basis for hiring, assembling, and motivating workplace teams. Going from the United States to Paris to Hong Kong has, he says, required him "to focus on employee needs in many different cultural settings."

Even in the United States, there's a vast difference in sociocultural dynamics between Orlando and Southern California. When I asked Greg how these geographical differences have influenced his approach to leadership, he replied, "Eighty percent of the time it's the same. It's about taking time with people." Acting on this commitment rather than just talking about it, he makes it a point to schedule time with his staff on a regular basis. But instead of setting agendas as he does in team meetings, Greg makes sure that the individual time he spends with his employees is all about them. "It's not my hour, it's theirs," he told me. "Taking time to focus on what's going on in their professional realm and what matters to *them* is one of the greatest equalizers between managers and employees. First of all it prevents isolation on both sides. Second, it demonstrates my commitment to their well-being."

Having now lived in several different countries, Greg told me, he has an even greater appreciation for inclusion as a leadership principle than ever before. For example, he said, "No matter how well I may learn to speak French, I'll never be French. It's impossible for me to view the world in the same way as people born into the French culture, but it's necessary for me to appreciate the differences associated with that experience in order to be successful in that environment." Hong Kong has given him an even greater perspective. In Paris, Greg noted, if he was just walking down the street, people might assume he was French. However, as a Caucasian, he will never be mistaken for Chinese while living and working in Hong Kong. It's exactly these types of personal experiences that he says have contributed to developing an even greater appreciation for human difference.

Recognizing the role his own identity plays in thriving as the perennial outsider, he continued, "I believe it's this same perspective, of not being the *same*, that's helped me develop and fine-tune my leadership skills that otherwise might have remained dormant. Perhaps out of necessity I've enhanced my success—no matter where in the world I find myself—because I've been blessed with the ability

I always seem to be coming into new environments as the *outsider*. That means I have to find effective ways to establish my own identity in order to be successful as a manager. Without question, being gay has contributed to my belief that all people are important; it's just part of who I am. For a manager, being able to focus on employees so they feel appreciated and valued shows that you're *interested*. I firmly believe this is my key to success. Of course, I'm also aided by an organization that allows me to lead to the best of my ability, which makes my commitment even stronger.

—Greg Morley

to see through the chaos and visualize a high-performing team where everyone is included and has an equal chance to succeed."

How Inclusion Affects Professional Relationships

When some people hear the word *relationships* applied to the workplace, they immediately start to think, "Oh great, now we're going to hear how we all need to get warm and fuzzy with the people we work with." A former colleague of mine calls it "Kumbaya time."

But that's mixing apples and oranges. While most of the basic dynamics apply to both personal and professional relationships, the manager-employee relationship centers on work. How is that different? In personal contexts, we need to know what a relationship is all about if we are to successfully function in the parameters of that friendship, romance, or committed partnership. We also need to know how our contribution to that relationship makes a difference to the other person. In the workplace, these dynamics simply take on a new agenda. The major difference is that, rather than both parties' sharing in the responsibility of providing each other with this type of information as in personal relationships, in organizations it's the sole responsibility of managers to provide their employees with answers to the following questions:

- What is the organization committed to and how do I fit in?
- How do these commitments apply to the daily processes of my work?
- Is my work making a difference?

It's interesting to note that these are also the same questions I hear from employees in other types of environments where management has little if any quality contact with their staff. What this suggests is that there is an across-the-board hunger among empowered employees for inclusion. To feel included, employees need these questions answered not just when they are hired or during annual reviews but on a continual basis. They need the answers if they are to experience the type of organizational relevance that leads to greater job engagement.

A 2005 study by the global consulting firm of BlessingWhite measured employees' attitudes and engagement levels, and found that only one-fifth of the nearly one thousand respondents surveyed believed their daily work was aligned with their manager's priorities and strategies. Only 21 percent of employees felt that they had "all the pieces in the engagement puzzle in place." Christopher Rice, BlessingWhite's CEO, said of the results, "If they're not engaged, employees are likely to be spinning, settling, or splitting."[4] The major finding of this study reveals that strong manager-employee relationships are linked to greater engagement among employees.[5] Without providing ongoing information to employees centered on these three questions, leaders are excluding their employees from the organization. Quite simply, when employees don't have the right answers, they aren't getting what they need from the manager-employee relationship.

Inviting Employee Engagement:
Steve Sears
Vice President, PepsiCo

Steve Sears is vice president of marketing for PepsiCo. He was hired out of the MBA program at Northwestern and has progressed upward to his current leadership role, where he's responsible for the marketing of the Pepsi trademark, in the course of an eighteen-year career at the company.

Ranked sixty-first on the Fortune 500 list, PepsiCo was one of the country's few large corporations to earn a perfect score on the Human Rights Campaign's corporate equality index (CEI). The CEI, a measurement tool calculating how inclusive Fortune 500 companies are toward their gay, lesbian, bisexual, and transgender employees, has become the industry standard for measuring GLBT equality. In the context of G Quotient leadership, it's relevant to note that all the Fortune 500 companies employing gay executives in this book scored a perfect or near-perfect score on those companies not scoring a perfect 100 percent, the on was the lack of inclusion for transgender employees rather than gay employees. Therefore, based on the parameters of my research, even the companies that fell short of perfect scores provided environments that on paper supported the professional development of gay employees.

The conviction that it's possible to use *inclusion* as a primary means to promote employee engagement is a belief that Steve shares with other G Quotient leaders. This belief contributes to the reasons why eight out of ten employees in G Quotient environments report that their managers regularly advocate for their best professional interests. From a leadership perspective, it's about the belief that individual success leads to organizational success.

In my research I found that gay executives believe that it's critical to the success of their organizations to provide an internal reality where inclusion is embraced as a positive driver of the workplace environment. On this subject, Steve told me, he's extremely sensitive to the need for modeling the type of inclusive behavior he wants to be the norm in his organization. "It really boils down to treating people the way you want them to treat you, which is simply to be *included*. I think gay people in particular know what it's like—even going back to childhood—not to be part of 'the group.' I have no doubt that's why I've made it a prior-

---

Relationships drive career success. As a manager, developing professional relationships with your employees—always based on mutual respect—drives *organizational* success. Getting results together is more important than just focusing on the raw results. There's a balance that needs to be struck between the process of work and the final product, which requires creating an environment that *invites* people to engage in their jobs. Of course, that invitation must apply to all employees.

—Steve Sears

ity in my own approach to leadership to learn about my employees as individuals."

Steve and I discussed how building relationships based on inclusion at work, particularly with employees, requires managers to believe in their own value as well as being authentic. On this subject, Steve shared his thoughts about what he believes is an "immense commitment to integrity and authenticity" that comes from being out and having gone through that process. He said, "It gives you the insight and security to use inclusion as a means of inviting employee motivation." This belief also speaks to the reason that so many employees with gay managers believe their bosses have their best professional interests at heart. It's about the belief that individual as well as organizational success results from the value of one's own personal identity.

Mark Twain once said, "Do not offer a compliment and ask for a favor at the same time. A compliment that is charged for is not valuable."[6] It's this exact type of message that Steve addresses when he talks about how professional relationships based on mutual respect drive organizational success. "At some point," he said, "managers are going to need that extra effort or extra commitment from their employees to get the job done." When you've consistently treated people fairly using respect and value as a catalyst, you'll find you have more than enough goodwill capital in the bank to meet whatever challenge may arise. According to Steve, "Inclusion creates a type of motivation that can't be ordered or forced— and when employee motivation is sincere, the commitment to superior performance is unparalleled."

Inclusion and Value

Hearing from people who have read something you've written, particularly when they've found it useful or enlightening, is truly rewarding. Because my work is about careers and leadership, sometimes people will write and ask for advice, sometimes they just need to sound off about whatever employment-related challenge they're dealing with at the moment. My career advice column on Walter Schubert's popular Gay Financial Network (www.gfn.com) came about because of the direct e-mail I received after writing several guest columns for the site. Hearing from so many different types of people is like having a special set of binoculars, because you get the chance to see beyond your own world into environments you would otherwise never get to know. One in particular stands out that I believe is exceptionally relevant to the principle of inclusion.

In late 2003, sitting in my office at USC, I received an e-mail note with a subject heading that read, "Gay Soldier/Iraq." My first thought was that it was some kind of promotion for a news item, but what I found was a very eloquent yet concise letter from an anonymous U.S. soldier deployed to Iraq. He said that he'd read an article online which quoted me on the subject of workplace equality, and how opportunities for gays and lesbians to be out and successful were improving every day. While appreciating the message, he wrote, "It has no real meaning to me in my current job."

We proceeded to exchange several rounds of e-mail over a relatively short time. Like many of the people who have written me, he needed an outlet to talk about his "job"—the difference being that his job involved life and death on a daily basis. To this day, I still don't know his name or much detail about what his life had been like before going to Iraq. He always e-mailed me from a Web-based account that was clearly separate from the one issued by the government. Primarily he talked about how it felt to be expected to put his life on the line every day for an employer that didn't value him enough as a human being to let him be who he is in the world. One message in particular was exceptionally profound, and speaks volumes about the impact of inclusion. He wrote, "Even though the people I work with think I'm part of their group, I'm not. You can't really be part of a group when you know you won't be treated with respect should you let them see the real you. That's why the respect they show me doesn't count. It's not real because they won't let *me* be real."

My decision to share this story in print isn't to debate the "don't ask don't tell" policy of the U.S. military. It's simply to illustrate how cut-off people feel from their employer and their coworkers when inclusion isn't the first principle of business leadership. Frankly, it doesn't matter whether you're employed by the U.S. military or a shoe factory. In the recalibrated world of work, *inclusion* is what drives successful leadership—and, as a result, successful organizations.

When the e-mail stopped, I wrote two more times with just a brief message of encouragement. I wanted him to know that someone with whom he had shared the "real him" hoped he remained safe and in one piece. I've never heard back, and of course I've always wondered whether he was injured, killed, or—in the best-case scenario—simply returned home. The other possibility is that he's just too afraid to send any more e-mail. When your employer doesn't respect or value you to the extent that your opportunities to succeed are based on your talents and skills as opposed to who you are as a human being, true meritocracy can never exist.

2

PRINCIPLE TWO: CREATIVITY

Creativity isn't a mystical gift only granted to a few special people. In organizations, creativity is the consequence of leadership that facilitates an environment designed to encourage and extract imagination. Is creativity more right-brain or left-brain? More gay than straight? The answer is that it's *both*.

Creativity, along with its cousin innovation, has become a standard buzzword in all types of organizations worldwide. While it's universally agreed that both are necessary for success in today's marketplace, it's difficult to get a consensus on the definition of either as a business term. More often than not, creativity and innovation are used as interchangeable idioms without a great deal of practical application, particularly when it comes to leadership.

In G Quotient environments, creativity is widely defined as the ability to look at ideas in fresh, new ways. Innovation is subsequently characterized as the *realization* of creativity. The gay executives represented in my research typically view creativity and innovation as separate but interdependent processes and products of their organization. In this respect, creativity is acknowledged as an employee *process* and innovation as an organizational *product*. In *Rise of the Creative Class*, Richard Florida describes creativity as the "ultimate economic resource," the key to raising both productivity and quality of life.[1] Building on that premise, it's logical to assume that our economic survival may very well rely on our ability to bridge creativity and innovation to *profitability*. How does

> *More than 91 percent of gay executives report that they frequently or always rely on brainstorming with their employees in order to develop new concepts that will give their organizations the competitive edge.*

that happen? Through leadership that incorporates creativity as one of its major principles.

At the beginning of 2000, the American Management Association surveyed five hundred CEOs around the country to answer one common question: "What must one do to survive in the twenty-first century?" While the practice of creativity was at the top of everyone's list, only 6 percent of CEOs reported that their organizations were doing a great job with it.[2] This rather startling fact leads me to believe that, for the most part, the widely stated commitment to pursuing creativity in organizations seems to be terribly misunderstood.

My own research indicates that one of the apparent causes for the short supply of creativity—and therefore of innovation—is a lack of understanding about what either actually means. Nor is there an understanding about how to implement and realize each as part of daily organizational life. Agreed, creativity and innovation can and should mean different things to different organizations depending upon field or industry. However, people in each of these environments still need a general recognition and consensus about their separate definitions if they are to make a positive contribution toward the achievement of organizational goals.

As a principle of G Quotient leadership, creativity facilitates forward organizational movement. I found that creativity in G Quotient environments centered on *concepts*, *possibilities*, and *people*, defined in the following manner:

- *Concepts:* Those original ideas that are imagined to develop or improve products, services, and the processes of work in an organization.

- *Possibilities:* The imagined potential of how these original ideas can become the basis for future success.
- *People:* The source for implementation of concepts and possibilities.

So how does creativity turn into innovation? For the majority of gay executives and their employees, the ability to put these three elements together in nonlinear ways represents the preferred route to innovation. John Sealy Brown, formerly chief scientist of the Palo Alto Research Center (PARC) for Xerox, believes the only way to proceed into the future evolves from "looking around," not from "looking ahead."[3] On this subject, one gay executive commented, "The level of creativity within any organization depends on how well it can envision its own future utilizing current resources."

Innovation in G Quotient environments stems from understanding the potential of the existing resources of creativity and using them effectively as fuel for achievement. When I thought about this particular perspective, I realized that one of the reasons only 6 percent of CEOs in the aforementioned study report that their organizations are doing a great job with creativity is that many people still think about creativity in terms of artistic relevance rather than as a business resource. In art, creativity is a function of original invention. While threads of this definition are valid in business, in formal organizational structures, creativity is much more about facilitation than about invention. In this sense, it's only through leadership facilitation that employees are given the encouragement, freedom, and guidance to look at ideas in fresh, new ways.

Eighty-eight percent of gay executives reported that they always believe it's important to recognize and make use of their employees' talents.

Imagining Possibilities:
Ralph Hexter
President, Hampshire College

Ralph Hexter is the fifth president of Hampshire College in Amherst, Massachusetts. He is one of the first non-closeted gay presidents in higher education and the first of a residential college in the United States. It's safe to say that Ralph's leadership ability has triumphed over any glass ceiling that otherwise might have kept him from joining the ranks of a very elite and select group of professionals—college presidents.

Speaking from my firsthand experience, the dynamics of a college campus can easily be likened to those in Washington, D.C. There are strong personal agendas, monumental egos, and some strategic maneuvering that I've seen rival the intrigue and power struggles played out on the Sunday morning political talk shows. However, instead of senators, congressional representatives, and lobbyists, there are deans, directors, and faculty. In this sense, much like the Oval Office at 1600 Pennsylvania Avenue, the office of college president is one of the most influential in our society. After all, it's in these institutions that the next generation of business and political leaders will discover and develop their talents and skills.

With an annual operating budget of $60 million, some 1,300 students, 110 full-time faculty, and approximately 275 staff, the Hampshire community (like most large organizations) is made up of seemingly countless personality types. To harness the talents, skills, and energy of such a large group of diverse employees, Ralph believes it's necessary to tap into the human process of creativity in order to realize the economic product of innovation.

Imagining how new concepts and possibilities can facilitate achievement has clearly played a role in Ralph's tremendous leadership success. As part of his professional belief system, his approach to leadership includes a conscious effort to develop environments that support and encourage employee creativity. Consequently, the extent of innovation realized by his organization begins with his

Creativity begins by imagining what's possible and what can be achieved. One of the basic tenets of my leadership is to use creativity to open the doors to individual as well as institutional accomplishment. Once you give people permission to imagine how their own abilities can make a positive difference, their commitment to whatever work-based initiative is required to make it happen will soar. Without the act of imagining, there can be no creativity.

—Ralph Hexter

own recognition that the imagining capability of employees is what also provides Hampshire with its own unique competitive edge.

During our interview, it became clear that Ralph has used his belief in imagining new concepts and possibilities to facilitate achievement in his own career. Prior to taking the number one job at Hampshire, he was executive dean of the College of Letters and Science at Berkeley, where his portfolio of responsibilities included financial administration, human resources, computing, and external relations, with eight hundred permanent faculty and five hundred staff members.

Like most G Quotient leaders, Ralph has escaped the boundaries set for him by society, because he imagined himself worthy of success and took professional action based on this belief. After receiving a bachelor's degree from Harvard, a master's from Oxford, and another master's and doctorate from Yale, he embodies a proven dedication to fostering one of his organization's foremost products—critical thinking.

I asked him how he begins this process. "I believe one of the most important skills any leader can have is the ability to *listen*." Without leadership that listens, he says, it's impossible for leaders to create environments that facilitate creativity and innovation, because listening creates professional meaning for employees. On this note, he perfectly articulated what creativity means in G Quotient

> Job engagement is something that happens naturally when people are excited about their work. In that respect, I believe, it's necessary to look at the interests and abilities of one's employees and then find new ways to create opportunities for them to get excited about how they contribute to the organization.
>
> —Ralph Hexter

environments: "My message is, 'Let me help *us* put our ideas into a form that makes our work more meaningful, more satisfying.'"

Managing Creativity

Warren Bennis, one of the world's most respected leadership gurus, once said, "In a Darwinian economy, only organizations that find ways to tap into the creativity of their members are likely to survive."[4] And in a highly competitive Darwinian economy where only the fittest survive, maximizing organizational creativity makes a significant contribution to sustained success—but maximizing organizational creativity goes beyond group exercises at annual retreats. Creativity in G Quotient environments factors into how managers think about their organizations, their employees, and the processes of work on a daily basis.

For creativity to become part of the daily working lives of all employees, managers must first commit to removing negativity from the workplace environment, which includes eliminating the chronic use of words such as *no, wrong,* and *never.* Gay executives make a deliberate choice to use language that promotes *Why we can* thinking instead of *Why we can't* that parallels the way they use language to model inclusion. Throughout all of my interviews with gay

Eighty-five percent of gay executives report that in their organizations, there is seldom or never too much time wasted on far-fetched or frivolous ideas.

executives, I consistently heard *us, our,* and *we* to describe the manager-employee relationship. It's a theme I later heard repeated in interviews with their employees.

Why is this important to developing a creative organization? It's impossible for creativity to rise to the surface in divisive environments. Going back to an earlier point, because G Quotient leadership essentially prevents "us against them" thinking, creativity has the opportunity to flourish because there's freedom to be open, curious, and even take risks when necessary. Quite simply, there's the freedom to imagine.

Gay Mitchell, executive vice president of strategic business development for the Royal Bank of Canada, which employs more than sixty thousand people worldwide, believes that in a knowledge-driven economy, companies must nurture creativity through a "compassionate yet performance-driven culture." Named one of Canada's most powerful women in 2004, she said that what was once considered to be the traditional soft people side of our business is now the new hard side.[5]

Regardless of how one defines soft and hard business skills, successful leaders have always been able to bring out the strengths of their employees. In G Quotient environments, encouraging employees to step out of their routines and take a chance on imagining and realizing a new kind of success results primarily from five management behaviors that bridge creativity to innovation. Across all four business sectors, I found that gay executives

- Define creativity in the context of the organization for everyone involved in the organization.
- Invite employees to imagine and brainstorm possibilities and ideas with management, colleagues, and professional groups.

> *Seventy-eight percent of gay executives report they always believe that when employees contribute to innovation in the organization, they feel connected and valued.*

- Affirm the value of creativity in the organization by reacting in a positive way to an employee's idea regardless of its potential.
- Guide employees in developing their ideas in a way that helps them gain confidence in their own creative abilities and align with the needs and values of the organization.
- Reward employees by implementing those ideas that will contribute to the forward movement of the organization while making effective use of available resources.

Bridging Creativity to Innovation:
Steven Tallman
Partner and Vice President, Bain & Company

Bain & Company is one of those organizations business students all around the country have at the top of their list when they begin to think about life after graduation. It's so desirable that one of my former students likened it to the seemingly out-of-reach black Centurion American Express card.

As leader of global operations for Bain & Company, Steven Tallman manages staff in thirty-one offices in twenty-one countries. Steven is the go-to executive for all knowledge, training, and technology functions for the firm. Beginning his career with Bain in 1986 as an associate consultant directly out of college, he has successfully climbed the corporate ladder, applying his own brand of creativity effectively each step of the way. Today, Steven divides his time between offices in San Francisco and The Netherlands, in addition to leading Bain's Capability Center in New Delhi. In the course of his impressive career at Bain, he has logged time in the firm's Tokyo, Moscow, London, Brussels, and Amsterdam offices.

> For me creativity is something natural and not something I consciously strive for. It's something that enters into all elements of my [leadership] style, but is most visible when finding better or more efficient ways to get things done.
>
> —Steven Tallman

I first met Steven when I was asked to moderate an executive panel at Reaching Out MBA. A few days before the event, I was given the contact information for the participants. I sent out e-mail to everyone on the list in an effort to discuss potential questions, and Steven was among the first to respond.

As a researcher, I have learned to save absolutely everything. I recently came across the notebook I used to write down some of the thoughts and perspectives of the folks who spoke on the panel. One of the notes I had under Steven's name read, "Creative freedom gives you the opportunity to capitalize on your personal strengths."

When I sent out invitations to participate in my research, once again, Steven was among the first to respond. As an organizational leader who manages employees all over the world, he told me, he believes everyone has the ability to be creative because everyone has personal strengths that when managed properly can fulfill that individual's potential. For Steven, fulfilling that potential has been part of his life since childhood. "As a kid I used to redesign Disneyland to optimize the park layout for fun. Today, I'm one of those people who can't walk into a Chinese take-out without having reengineered the entire operation in my head before I have even ordered."

When I asked him how that ability affects his approach to leadership, he said, "It has played a tremendous role in my professional life, because I have used something that comes natural to me as a career strength. One of the things that I believe is critical to good management is finding those natural abilities in my employees and encouraging them to develop them as career strengths." Steven said that creativity has a lot to do with his own ability to recognize these potential strengths among his employees. "I believe I have a knack for seeing abilities in people that they may not see themselves, or at least have yet to discover. Perhaps it is more difficult to see our own talents, but good managers can spot talent and good leaders can develop that talent."

As a result of working in organizations where creativity is a principle of leadership, employees of gay executives report greater professional inspiration due to environments that value creative freedom. Overall, employees in G Quotient environments across all four business sectors report increased opportunities for promotion and advancement as a result of their own creative freedom. Last but not least, they report that creativity makes their work more enjoyable. As we all know, when we enjoy doing something, our engagement in the process is accordingly high. It is why career counselors always ask their clients about favorite hobbies and how they spend their free time when helping them identify their natural talents.

When I told Steven that employees in G Quotient environments identified creativity as a significant contributor to greater job engagement, it was something he already knew. "I give my staff a lot of flexibility in how they manage their areas, but I do guide them to think creatively on how we can do things better, more efficiently, and with greater expediency. It is really about using creativity to work smarter." From a leadership perspective, it's one of the ways Steven has successfully managed creativity. From an organizational perspective, it's the genesis of innovation.

Becoming Inspired by Creativity

Max DePree, the famous chairman emeritus of furniture giant Herman Miller, once said, "The visible signs of artful leadership are expressed, ultimately, in its practice."[6] The search for future success starts with leadership that recognizes the extent of its own creative capital as well as that represented by each employee. It's this existing asset that ultimately yields innovation and profitability in all types of organizations. In this sense, think of it as the outcome of all professional endeavors being predetermined by the imagining that goes into their creation and development.

I taught theories of career development at USC for six years before joining the Marshall School of Business to teach business communication, and I am sure that possessing a natural curiosity about how and why people choose professions and make career choices is a prerequisite for the job. One of the truths that I've found over the years of studying why some people are successful and others are not lies in the personal discovery of something called transferable talents. Basically, it's identifying those career strengths that Steven talked about, which can serve as threads of success over a professional lifetime, even if you completely change career fields.

When I interviewed Roland Jarquio (whose profile appears in Chapter Six to help illustrate the principle of intuition), this very subject of transferable talents immediately became part of our conversation. His own experience in identifying creativity as one of his own threads of success provides practical insight into what it means to be inspired by creativity. Talking about his experience at the global consulting firm of McKinsey & Company, he said, "A competitive advantage I had at McKinsey was having a sense of how important creativity was in relationship to my own achievement within the firm. It wasn't that I was right-brained and everyone else was left-brained. For me, the more accurate term would be *whole-brained*. Everything I did, even the most basic PowerPoint chart, had to be inspired by my own brand of creativity, from visual presentation to style of writing."

This highly practical definition illustrates what instilling creativity into the life stream of an organization really means. It's about using creativity to influence and improve all work-related activities. Among gay executives, the practice of creativity as a principle of leadership plays a major role in setting themselves, their employees, and their organizations apart from mediocrity. There's a demonstrated and acknowledged need to be what many described as "better than the rest." As a collective group, striving for the extraordinary has contributed to what could easily qualify as "artful leadership." They successfully navigate today's recalibrated world of work by recognizing that creativity as a leadership principle is a leading source of success—for leaders themselves, their employees, and the organization.

Using Creativity to Stand Apart:
Mike Fuller
Vice President, IBM Global Services

Mike Fuller has been with IBM for more than sixteen years and has managed staffs ranging in number from twelve to more than twelve hundred. In his current role as a vice president in IBM's Global Services unit, Mike devotes most of his time to business transformation outsourcing (BTO), developing long-term strategies for key partnerships and alliances. These alliances play a central role in the development and execution of deals with some of the world's largest corporations. Each typically represents a commitment of seven to ten years between IBM Global Services and the client, with budgets often exceeding $1 billion. Essentially, corporations will outsource entire business units (such as Human Resources or Finance, for example) to IBM's BTO unit to redesign, streamline, and then run the processes of that particular unit, with the goal of increasing their competitive advantage in the marketplace while implementing successful change and optimizing cost-effectiveness. From Finance to Human Resources to Technology, Mike's work reaches across all types of fields and organizational functions.

Because of Mike's expertise in transformation strategies, I originally thought our interview would most likely fit well in the chapter on adaptability. After all, transformation is about change. But effective transformation in the twenty-first century also requires creativity. It's a commitment that's proven successful for Mike in his own work as well as in his approach to leadership.

In his own career, Mike told me, his personal level of confidence has been enhanced due to the commitment at IBM to LGBT diversity. IBM was the first major company of its stature to establish a dedicated LGBT sales team to reach out to this segment of the marketplace, and today this team reports directly to Mike. "In my early days with the company, while I wouldn't describe myself as closeted, I wasn't really out. IBM was one of the first corporations

Creativity requires confidence. I believe we all have the capability to be creative, but not necessarily the confidence to fully exploit our own vision and talents. To be a successful manager, it's vital to instill confidence in your employees in such a way that it enables them to recognize and take advantage of their own creative abilities. I often assign projects to people that I know will challenge and stretch them beyond what they think they are capable of doing. It may mean that you have to commit additional time to provide support and resources in order for them to succeed, but the payoff is tremendous. Once people realize they *can* do something they didn't think possible, their confidence level soars. It's that resulting confidence that unlocks the doors to creativity. It's management through empowerment.

—Mike Fuller

to structure diversity around the idea of talent, and when I found out that included gay employees, it made a tremendous difference to me as a human being." It's one of the reasons why, in addition to his other professional responsibilities, Mike leads the LGBT sales team. "When I first got involved with IBM's LGBT diversity efforts, I found that I became more visible, which led to new types of professional opportunities in the company."

IBM was also a pioneer in establishing a nondiscrimination policy for LGBT employees, which Mike believes has had a direct and positive impact on the organization's creativity.

"When you think about how organizations can unleash employee creativity, it has a great deal to do with constructing an environment where people can be honest. When you remove organizational pressure to accept or conform to societal prejudice or bias, you empower people to put their full effort into their work. Employees will always make a greater impact on an organization being themselves." It's a philosophy that appears to be working. In 2004, IBM filed more new U.S. patents than any other company, a tangible measure of organizational creativity.

Innovation occurs at the intersection where diverse people are brought together. It's where creativity comes naturally. That's why creativity depends on assembling teams where these intersections can occur. Otherwise, the outcome will always be homogenous and lack the creativity demanded in a knowledge economy.

—Mike Fuller

When it comes to nurturing creativity, Mike sees his leadership role in two ways. The first is to be an "executive cheerleader." He believes it's necessary to the success of individual employees as well as the greater organization to guide and encourage people in realizing their own creative potential. It's why Mike assigns projects that require employees to stretch themselves professionally as a way to conquer new frontiers and gain confidence. Second, Mike told me, he believes it's his role to remove the corporate bureaucracy and roadblocks that can often get in the way of the creative process. "When people are preoccupied with red tape, they risk losing their creative focus." Mike said that one of the benefits of achieving a certain level of success in an organization is the accompanying opportunity it often affords to cut through the red tape: "It's my goal to remove those barriers so my team has the time and energy to fully pursue their creative talents."

Mike also told me he's a firm believer in allowing his employees to perform their job without the burden of having to look over one shoulder all the time. He said there is no quicker way to stifle creativity than to micromanage your employees. "To start with, I do my best to hire people who have proven track records or, if they're just beginning their careers, who demonstrate great potential." Mike commented that constantly monitoring the work of capable people is an insult to their skills. "I don't believe that making a mistake is always a terrible thing. Rather than berating someone over what has already happened, it's imperative to pitch in and help your employees make the necessary corrections while 'guiding' them to acquire the type of knowledge that prevents it from happening again in the future. It's how expertise is born."

3

PRINCIPLE THREE: ADAPTABILITY

Adaptability is ultimately about being flexible enough to change. As a principle of leadership, *adaptability* represents the willingness and capacity of executives to make organizational modifications deemed necessary as a result of change, often the direct result of creativity and innovation. However, it's not about adapting to change simply for the sake of being different, it's about how these modifications support and advance organizational success. It's a critical part of G Quotient leadership because in the recalibrated workplace, shifting employee needs and demographics, along with globalization and rapidly evolving technologies, continue to bring about dramatic changes in both the perceptions and processes surrounding the meaning of work on what seems like an hourly basis.

In G Quotient environments, adaptability is widely recognized as a behavioral goal for both managers and employees.

As a result, it's important to address the meaning of and appreciation for change in these settings. As a noun, *change* can be defined as the process of alteration. As a verb, it speaks to the active facilitation of transformation or even, in some cases, revolution. Therefore, pursuing and embracing change in the context of an organization makes a significant impact on the individual perceptions of both managers and employees. Why? Because in order to realize all of the benefits that can result from adapting to change, *change itself* must take on a positive meaning within the workplace environment.

It's not necessary to go any further than opening a window or door to see a firsthand example of that old cliché, "The only constant

> *Among gay executives, 95 percent report that they frequently or always enjoy keeping their organizations on the move and adapting to the times.*

about the universe is change." Nature in all of its glory and sometimes fury is a daily reminder of the benefits of constant change. The human body itself is in a perpetual flux or state of change. It's an interesting paradox that while many people prefer consistent routines and predictability, neither nature nor the human body are ever static. This brings practical relevance to the concept that change also brings renewal. Like nature and the human body, organizations cannot be successful in states of perpetual monotony. As a principle of leadership, adaptability to change facilitates a necessary connection between gay executives and the constantly evolving business realities of their organizations.

One of the greatest challenges related to the recalibrated workplace has to do with managers' identifying how technological as well as economic, social, and political change requires organizational flexibility. Fear of the unknown makes many managers hesitant participants in the evolution of their own organizations. However, adaptability and flexibility have great meaning, because change affects everyone in the organization.

For any organization to run at peak levels, everyone in the working environment must view change as a constructive force for organizational health—or run the risk of professional extinction. I found that gay executives recognize that they live in an instantly connected global society, one where distant events can have an immediate effect on entire industries worldwide. As a collective group they tend to like the idea that their organizations are in a constant state of ebb and flow. In fact, it's this appreciation for "ebb and flow" that many believe is a great contributor to the development of a healthy and productive organization.

To continue with an earlier metaphor, in nature, a balanced ebb and flow is having an overabundance of rainfall along with not enough.

It's about variation. Among the foremost benefits of this type of variation cited by gay executives and their employees are the prevention of groupthink and the enhancement of employee engagement and commitment to excellence. So how can the potential for constant change be beneficial? From a management perspective, it represents the potential for greater organizational achievement. From an employee perspective, an environment that is always ready to adapt to change increases the opportunity for pursuing new opportunities, which directly coincides with people's need for individual value. One employee told me, "Adapting to changes before our competitors always puts us in front of new trends and learning curves. It makes me feel like I have the chance to put my footprint on the future of our industry."

Among the gay executives I interviewed, the need to be what was often described as "better than the rest" played more than a small role in their readiness to adapt to change. It's also in alignment with what I learned in my undergraduate business studies: no matter how accomplished you are, there's no room for resting on past accomplishments. From an entrepreneur's perspective, which I found mirrored by the gay executives identified in my research, new, better, and improved ways of doing things are always waiting on the horizon. I never once recall hearing any of my professors in the entrepreneur program say, "Well, that's just how we've always done it." In G Quotient environments, there are always new and better ways to accomplish organizational objectives.

A Representative of Change:
David White
Senior Consultant, Deloitte Consulting LLP

David White is a senior manager in the Human Capital practice at Deloitte Consulting in Los Angeles. As a member firm of the global organization Deloitte Touche Tohmatsu, known in business circles simply as "Deloitte," Deloitte Consulting is part of Deloitte & Touche USA, the American parent of all Deloitte practices in the states.

With more than six years of progressive success with the firm, David specializes in the integration of people issues with business strategy. The organization is the second-largest HR consultancy in the world, and its mission is to enhance the performance, productivity, and profitability of its clients, which include some of the world's largest corporations.

As a senior manager in the consulting field, David finds that leadership always represents the potential for change; the team of employees that he manages changes from engagement to engagement. He assembles a new team for each assignment, based on the client's needs. In a world of constant transformation, he has demonstrated more than just an understanding of the meaning of change. He's been able to successfully adapt to all its effects and implications and thus enhance not just his own success but the success of his clients and employees, and, of course, his employer.

David told me that one of the reasons he was attracted to consulting as a career field was the idea that it was a profession that would never stagnate. "In consulting, being able to deal with change is a requirement of the job. The very nature of consulting is about constant change simply because you're never on the same engagement twice. My career depends on change."

He joined the firm at a time when the Internet was changing businesses all over the world, and he told me that operating in a knowledge economy has unquestionably changed his field. "Today, clients have access to vast amounts of information, and are therefore constantly exposed to all types of business practices and ideas from

> Going into new environments all the time means that I have to quickly adapt to new surroundings. For me, it's energizing. Knowing that I'm going to have to roll with anything the client throws at me is one of the things I look forward to every day when I go to work. As a manager, I work hard to pass on my own appreciation for change to my team. It's why we're there.
>
> —David White

across town to across the ocean." Prior to the Internet and pervasive access to industry-specific information, consultants had the primary responsibility of educating clients about new business strategies that could improve and enhance their organizations. Certainly that's still a major part of the consultant's role, but there's a new emphasis on how to help clients manage and sift through all that information to figure out what's right for their own organizations.

David told me that as a result of such pervasive access to industry-specific information, the goals of today's clients are always subject to change. According to David, "[That] makes it necessary to be open to a shift in directions, sometimes even in the middle of an engagement. When you're in a leadership role, it's critical to your success to adapt to these changes and recognize that modification is often what makes the difference between good and great."

Because gay executives build environments that embrace change, employees are often asked to adapt their approach to job performance in order to maximize effectiveness and meet organizational goals. This is exactly what David described when he talked about being open to a "shift in directions." In G Quotient environments, the value of this belief extends to employees as well. Employees know that if a light bulb suddenly goes on about how to perform their job better, their managers are open to adapting the processes of work— again, to support and advance organizational success.

When I asked David if he thought being gay has had any impact on his success as a representative of change, I could tell by his voice that my question almost seemed unnecessary. "Most definitely," he replied. "When you're growing up and figuring out who you are, you learn to adapt to society because you think that you're the one who needs to change. But then you realize that living a truthful life shouldn't require you to change, and you begin to adapt to the reality that some people in this world are going to have a problem with that decision." In this sense, David says, "That's why gay people are comfortable living with a certain amount of ambiguity. The answers weren't always there, so you learn to turn that into an advantage."

Accepting Ambiguity

Alvin Toffler, the American writer and futurist, foretold in his early work that the migration to an Information Age would force change on human culture with unparalleled acceleration.[1] Truly, in today's business landscape, that migration has in fact made information itself a standard measurement of economic value. In this sense, many measurements of value associated with twentieth-century business as well as leadership paradigms are becoming less and less significant. In fact, it could be argued that they are becoming liabilities. For example, in some organizations, valuation of assets is based less on physical capital than on intellectual capital—even though, for many managers, assets that can't be touched or seen have no value. That's why accepting ambiguity in the twenty-first century is becoming a business necessity.

Accepting ambiguity and being comfortable with fuzzy or hazy information allows gay executives to stay in the moment, evaluate information from a fresh perspective, and be able to move in any direction that may be appropriate for the situation or event.

Being comfortable with ambiguity opens up worlds of professional possibilities because it gives people permission to see connections that might otherwise not be recognized or entertained as viable business options. For example, if managers aren't willing to adapt to change, it's unlikely that in today's marketplace they'll be able to identify and build new strategies that will take them any further than they already are. Quite simply, being able to accept ambiguity as a satisfactory or even desirable state of organizational being appears to prevent G Quotient environments from getting stuck.

Eastern cultures have traditionally viewed change as a key to living a long and successful life. Studies now confirm the positive link between adaptability to change and living into one's eighties, nineties, and even past a hundred years of age. While genetics certainly play a large role in determining who has the potential to reach triple-digit age, research documents that getting stuck in the past is definitely *not* a recipe for successful old age. Nor is it a recipe for successful leadership. Gay executives widely recognize that the dynamics associated with change represent new opportunities to examine and reexamine the processes of work and how they fit into organizational goals on a daily basis. If you've ever worked in an organization that's trapped in the past, you'll immediately know what I mean. Several years ago I was advising a very accomplished man who had been at the same engineering firm for several years. He said to me, "Everyone in the organization walks around like zombies."

In the majority of environments, chronic repetition leads to disengagement and low morale. Repeating the same conversations and exact processes of work over and over inhibits forward movement not just for managers and employees but for the organization itself. One of the organizational benefits associated with ambiguity in relationship to G Quotient environments lies in what can best be termed *yet-to-be-discovered* information. Because there's an acknowledged respect for discovery in G Quotient leadership, I found it less likely for gay executives to make hasty decisions. Rather than just accepting what might be most evident at the moment, they display a decided commitment to searching for new choices and solutions.

Adapting to New Ways of Doing Business:
Bob Page
President and Founder, Replacements, Ltd.

The son of a tobacco farmer, Bob Page grew up in a family of six in a three-room house in rural North Carolina. Today, he's president of Replacements, Ltd., a company he founded almost twenty-five years ago that now has annual sales exceeding $70 million. Replacements is one of those companies you might not hear about until you need them. And once you do, you of course marvel at the genius of its concept. As the world's largest seller of new and used dinnerware, including china, crystal, and silver, Bob's company is a magnet for people all over the globe who need to replace broken or missing pieces in their own collections. More than ten thousand calls per day come into its headquarters in Greensboro, North Carolina, so it's evident that once people do find out about Replacements, they immediately tell all their friends, relatives, and neighbors.

Bob, who describes his 550 employees as an "extended family," has a personal commitment to know every employee on a first-name basis. And it pays off; Replacements was named by *Fast Company* as one of the "Fast 50 Companies" in 2004. It has also made *Carolina Parenting Magazine*'s list of the best companies to work for every year since 2003, because of its family-friendly policies and procedures, which include adoption assistance, financial aid programs, and on-site counselors, as well as a personal leave program that allows employees time off to deal with family issues. I believe it's safe to say that finding a company honored by *Carolina Parenting Magazine* that also scores a perfect 100 percent on HRC's Corporate Equality Index is not an everyday occurrence. Like Mitchell Gold and Bob Williams, as an out-of-the-closet gay business owner in the South, Bob Page has built leadership that has transcended the conservative ideologies long associated with the region to become one of the most sought-after employers in the state.

When you talk to Bob, it's immediately clear he believes that having the kind of organizational culture where employee-centered programs and benefits improve the quality of life for his employees also creates an environment that's more engaged, productive, and, as he says, *happier*. In fact, early in our interview I was certain that his commitment to inclusion would be the primary focus of our conversation. But that thought quickly changed as soon as I shared my findings about gay executives and their ability as organizational leaders to successfully adapt to change.

When Bob quit his job as an accountant in 1981 to pursue life as an entrepreneur, it obviously represented a dramatic change in his life. He was the first college graduate in his family, and he shared with me his parents' apprehension about his heading off down a new professional road. Despite all the ambiguity and unknowns that come with making such a bold move, what Bob did know was that he

Since starting Replacements, Ltd., in 1981, my belief in the value of change has always been a constant leadership ideal. It has enabled me to take what was essentially a long-time hobby and turn it into a $70 million a year business. For me, change is synonymous with improvement. It's about looking for better ways to do business, and that means providing superior customer service and offering a great place for employees to work. Today more than ever, if you have your head and feet stuck in the past, you become a dinosaur. It's nearly impossible to stay in business without recognizing the tremendous role that change plays in the growth and longevity of any business.

—Bob Page

wanted to do "something fun for a living," and making a change was the only way to achieve this goal. Aside from having to be adaptable on a personal level to be able to deal with the resulting ambiguity associated with trading in a steady paycheck to work out of his attic, Bob has also been able to take advantage of his own ability to adapt to change in order to take full advantage of running a business in the Digital Age.

Since 2000, Replacements, Ltd. has markedly changed the way it reaches out to and serves its global customers. Today, half of its business is conducted online. Going from a million pieces of mail per month to just half that amount, under Bob's leadership the company has not only cut its sizable printing and mailing expenses but expanded business and improved its already high level of customer service. Bob told me, "Customers love being able to get instant information about our products. It's what all businesses talk about but few deliver." He said, "There was no question that we wouldn't adapt to all of the new possibilities that existed for us as a company. It represented our future." In fact, one of Bob's employees told me that he never wants to work where the "status quo is good enough."

In *Martin Chuzzlewit*, Charles Dickens wrote, "Change begets change. Nothing propagates faster."[2] When I asked Bob why he thought so many organizations always seem to be "catching up" rather than leading, he noted that if people in management don't view change as a positive catalyst for their business, they will never see all the successful possibilities it might bring. Because change happens so fast, without management's commitment to see, understand, and adapt to its potential effects, the pure momentum of change often leaves the organization behind.

Bob's ability to recognize change as a catalyst for success has taken his company to new heights. As a principle of leadership, adaptability to change requires that leaders recognize how their own effectiveness is fundamentally linked to embracing change, being comfortable with ambiguity, and challenging the status quo. It also requires leaders to do more than just be ready for change; it requires them to *act* on change. Those who don't will always be catching up.

Nonconformity and Flexibility

The majority of gay executives interviewed for this book are comfortable with professional risk taking, and they share a belief in the usefulness of nonconformity. When you put these two elements together they combust to challenge the status quo. One executive remarked that perhaps it was because it was just himself and his partner, he didn't have to worry that breaking new ground in his career might somehow impact a child's college fund or destabilize family economics. Whether or not it's due to a greater sense of financial independence, the professional payoff for being comfortable about challenging the status quo has unquestionably played a role in the ability of gay executives to adapt to change easily. In my research, I found that more than 85 percent of employees reporting to gay managers state that people who challenge the status quo are valued within their working environment.

With that said, it's important to note that in G Quotient environments, challenging the status quo isn't about questioning the significance of every existing practice and procedure. I was once at a conference where this behavior was referred to as the "Don Quixote syndrome," where people are always fighting windmills and nothing ever gets done because of impractical objectives. Rather, in G Quotient environments, challenging the status quo is about identifying, selecting, and pursuing those changes that offer the greatest organizational reward. In this sense, I found gay executives to represent the opposite of what "fighting windmills" has come to mean, because it's about doing rather than dreaming. And doing requires feasibility in addition to flexibility.

In G Quotient environments, flexibility takes on two forms, *cognitive* and *experiential*. The cognitive form is about recognizing that adapting to change always has the potential to improve the forward movement of an organization or working unit. It's about what's inside an employee's mind and how that employee views adaptability as a positive influence on work. The experiential aspect is about being flexible in one's actual job performance so as to accommodate change. It's about approaching and doing one's work in a new and better way, because of technological advances, research discoveries, or other breakthroughs that affect specific fields and industries.

Leo Tolstoy, the great Russian author of such classics as *War and Peace* and *Anna Karenina,* once said, "Everyone thinks of changing the world, but no one things of changing himself." As a leadership principle, adaptability to change is an exceptionally personal endeavor. For example, both cognitive and experiential flexibility are highly individual responses. Over the years, I have witnessed some excellent change efforts go down in flames because management had no appreciation for addressing the minds and hearts of the organization's employees as a first step toward change. There is no faster way to get the wheels to fly off a new initiative or project than failing to personally involve employees in the development and implementation of organizational change.

In those G Quotient environments that have undergone radical transformations, change didn't occur overnight. Their leadership made a conscious effort to implement change over a period of

> *Sixty-four percent of gay executives seldom or never believe that their organizations run smoothest using tried-and-true processes and procedures.*

time that coincided with the level of flexibility—both cognitive and experiential—of the organization's employees. However, it's clearly the responsibility of organizational leaders to create environments where flexibility is favorably embraced.

Challenging the status quo, embracing change, being comfortable with ambiguity, and flexibility are all interrelated concepts of the leadership principle of adaptability. For gay executives, my research suggests, these concepts aren't as much theoretical ideals as they are the practical result of what I have already described as being in the world in a different way since childhood. As a collective group of concepts, I found them to also contribute to a strong sense of professional independence. To better understand why, I would simply suggest going back to what David White said, "The answers weren't always there." Because gay executives often found themselves having to create their own path in life, they have a greater sense of freedom to create an equally original path in their approach to organizational leadership.

4

PRINCIPLE FOUR: CONNECTIVITY

G Quotient environments are assembled, supported, and advanced through a unique professional network of *connectivity*. In relationship to the G Quotient paradigm, connectivity follows adaptability because change regularly mandates the need to acquire new perspectives and professional tools in order to succeed based on new conditions and contexts. As it's defined in this chapter, connectivity keeps executives and their employees constantly in touch with organizational and industry movement, helping them reach and maintain a competitive advantage. In application, connectivity in G Quotient environments takes on two forms: external networking and internal awareness.

External networking begins with the immediate organization or working unit serving as the hub of its own networking system. As a result of having greater autonomy, employees in G Quotient environments are encouraged to link to all types of external information, resources, and people to equip themselves with new knowledge so they can maximize their responsiveness to change. Several employees in these environments specifically noted that having the freedom to connect with the resources or people they need to do a better job empowered them to be successful. It also increased opportunities for professional advancement because it added to their individual level of expertise. In other words, connectivity was perceived to enhance their abilities while adding to their résumés.

The other form of connectivity in G Quotient environments is what I define as *internal awareness*. It's an ability to connect various types of realities within the organization so as to maximize effectiveness. For example, connecting employees to the right job or even to the right resources and people represents how this form of connectivity promotes success. Among the gay executives in my research, I found that this awareness includes an honest recognition of their own talents and skills. Several gay executives told me that good leaders should never get trapped into thinking they have to be experts at everything. Instead, beyond recognizing and appreciating their professional strengths, I was told, it's vital to the success of their organizations to also connect with the realities of their own professional weaknesses. It's this personal type of internal awareness that I found contributed to gay executives' hiring the right people to augment and complement their own abilities. The result: a more balanced organization, equipped to succeed at all levels.

Even though the term *connectivity* has developed a lot of traction in the last decade relative to the Internet, the concept and practicality of connectivity really isn't all that new. Going back several hundred years, seventeenth-century English poet John Donne coined that famous phrase, "No man is an island." In my own research, I found that gay executives believe their organizations cannot be effective as islands, and they need to continually draw from outside reservoirs if they are to succeed. One executive told me, "Leaders who believe they are all-knowing and run their organizations as stand-alone hierarchies will soon be standing alone—in the unemployment line."

Researchers and social scientists often draw comparisons between social networks and the Worldwide Web. Even the words *Worldwide* and *Web* speak to our movement as a society away from linear, stand-alone hierarchies toward more interconnected and flattened networks that extend far beyond our immediate environment. A spider's web is one of those often-used analogies that describes the interconnection and intricacies of a connected world. Like you, I've read countless articles and books devoted to this particular analogy. However, I recently gained a new appreciation for its accuracy while taking my dog Winston out for a nature call. While waiting for him to take care of business under his favorite tree, I noticed that the tree had become an anchor to what could easily be described as the world's largest spider web. It was certainly the largest web I'd ever encountered. Spun between two trees, it was at least six feet across and just as tall. Because I happened to be standing edgewise rather than facing this imposing web, I was immediately struck by its flatness. Simply because of its sheer size, the experience was like looking at a spider's web for the first time. Perhaps because it was the noon hour and the sun was at its peak, I could clearly see why it has become such a universal analogy. It's truly a giant network of interconnection.

That afternoon while taking a break from my work, I entered the key words "spider web" and "network" into a search engine just to see what it would return. One of the links, which was actually a site devoted to the study of spiders, addressed the practicality of the web's connectivity and its flatness. In great detail, the article described how the spider, even if located at the opposite side of the web, knows at once when a bug has flown into its domain, because the web's connectivity is such that it immediately alerts the spider that there is new movement in the environment. The connection between this phenomenon of nature and G Quotient leadership leapt to mind. What crystallized for me was how the spider's survival depends on its ability to set up an environment that keeps it in touch with change so that it can quickly take action. In G Quotient environments, it's this same network of connectivity that empowers gay executives to know when change has occurred so they can act quickly and efficiently. It's connectivity that keeps everyone in touch with new movement—in their own environments as well as in their fields and industries.

From a historical perspective, gay men have created networks of connectivity for the same reason spiders create theirs—as a means of survival. From West Hollywood to the Castro district in San Francisco to Greenwich Village, gay men successfully created their own networks of connectivity, building relationships that ensure community. For decades, it was only in these urban connected communities that gay men were able to be out of the closet and live authentically.

This is one of the major reasons, as I stated earlier in the Introduction, that gay men were able to pull together community-based resources almost overnight to provide services, comfort, and solutions for early AIDS patients in their community. *Connectivity* facilitated this rapid mobilization process, and in the recalibrated workplace, it's become a principle of leadership that is now contributing to the success of gay executives in business.

Connecting Employees to Success:
Brent Mitchell
Senior Vice President, CitiCapital

Brent Mitchell is a senior vice president at CitiCapital, a business unit of Citigroup, headquartered in Mt. Laurel, New Jersey. Since joining the company in 2000 as a result of a corporate merger, Brent has received several promotions, rising from vice president of business development for the company's Healthcare and Energy Group to senior vice president and chief of staff of the same organization. In fact, the week of our interview, he accepted the position of senior vice president and business segment head for the entire Healthcare and Energy Group.

Beginning his career in a family business where he was out of the closet in an affirming environment, Brent set the stage early on for building a professional life based on his own individual value. Today, he attributes much of his leadership success to being authentic in his personal as well as professional life. "Being out, I think I approach management with a different set of glasses than someone might who is straight—or even gay but still in the closet. The last thing I want an employee to feel is that they're separated from themselves or their real life at work. That's directly related to my own life experiences. I truly want their work to be a meaningful part of their life rather than something that's a necessary evil. I want them to succeed."

With more than $20 billion of assets and three hundred thousand customers, CitiCapital is among the top commercial finance companies in the United States. As the parent company of CitiCapital,

Citigroup ranked eighth on the 2005 Fortune 500 list and scores a perfect 100 percent rating on HRC's Corporate Equality Index. It's another example of how inclusion results in profitable organizations. It also speaks to why gay executives like Brent are thriving as organizational leaders in these inclusive companies.

Numerous studies have documented how positive work-based relationships with peers as well as supervisors produce feelings of belonging and loyalty to the organization. When I brought up this subject, Brent echoed a sentiment expressed by other G Quotient leaders. "Relationships at any level are certainly the result of human connection. But in terms of the workplace, there's also a limit to how far you can go in any organization without friends." One of the things we discussed was the difference between social friendships and professional friendships. While Aristotle described the perfect friendship as "that between good men who are alike in excellence or virtue," professional friendships are formed primarily to work together toward like goals.[1] For Brent, professional friendships must be based on mutual respect if they are to be meaningful relative to shared goals. He said, "It's imperative for employees to know they

As a manager, I've always believed there are three chief connections that must happen in order to be a successful leader. First, it's critical for managers to be connected to their own strengths and weaknesses, and be affirming of both. Second, it's imperative to connect employees with the right job, otherwise the organizational framework itself will be weak. Third, by connecting your employees to the right job, you facilitate a subsequent connection between people and their own career aspirations. In this sense, it's vitally important for managers to understand where their employees want to go in order to place them in positions that are moving them in the right direction. When people are managed to be forward-moving, they will always care about their work and its quality, because there's something personal at stake—their own future.

—Brent Mitchell

are just as important as you are in the relationship. These types of professional friendships convey a sense of appreciation for an employee's well-being and that's essential to engagement. For me, it isn't something I sit down and consciously think about, it's just something I do day-to-day."

Norman Cousins, for more than forty years the legendary editor of the *Saturday Review*, once said, "A book is like a piece of rope; it takes on meaning only in connection with the things it holds together." In Brent's organization, connectivity takes on a deeper meaning because of what it holds together. Connectivity keeps his employees attuned to new movement in their professional realm. It's this resulting awareness that makes G Quotient environments more current, more competitive, and more successful in the Digital Age.

How Connectivity Creates Meaning

Studies that examine work-related stress invariably find that lack of time is always a leading cause. In a downsized world, having enough time to do everything we want or even need to do requires all of us to work with greater purpose and meaning. A 2003 study cited by *Work and Family Newsbrief* in December of that year reported that 47 percent of employees polled by LifeCare, one of the largest privately owned employee benefits organizations in the United States, cited time management as the number one source of stress in their lives. When faced with overwhelming demands on their professional time, many people react by removing themselves from the fray. They choose to hole up in their offices, with the idea that they will create greater meaning when they are alone. However, in the digital age, *meaning* requires connectivity.

Consider how many aspects of your life are facilitated via who or what you are connected to in the world. For Gen Y, being connected is in fact how they create meaning. In this sense, it's become the social equivalent of oxygen. Without the instant opportunity to pull a breath of metaphorical air from their respective networks, connecting to friends, family, and even information-based resources for school or work, they respond by feeling something that resembles suffocation as opposed to mere isolation. Just try taking away any college student's cell phone, now equipped with instant messaging, Internet access, and camera and video capability as standard features, and you'll see a look of emptiness that's worthy of a Cecil B. DeMille close-up. For myself, if my e-mail goes down even for a few minutes, I feel less vital. When it's taken away, I become temporarily immobilized. Most interesting is just how quickly we've grown dependent on our need for connection, demanding faster, greater, and more pervasive access. Today, being meaningful and creating meaning for others depends on connectivity. Why? Because connectivity is empowering.

Bringing Connectivity Forward:
James Stofan
Executive Director, University of California

James Stofan is executive director of alumni affairs and protocol for the University of California, the largest public university system in the United States. UC represents ten campuses, including Berkeley and UCLA. It also boasts more than 1.4 million alumni worldwide. In his leadership role, James connects UC alumni all over the world. In the field of higher education, alumni executives are often described as "friend-raisers" rather than fundraisers. But the importance of this role goes beyond social connections. All colleges and universities recognize the business impact associated with having engaged alumni, because collectively alumni represent a primary source of financial support. James's job is one that ultimately provides long-term security for the institution itself.

James has devoted the majority of his distinguished career—which spans thirty years in higher education—to alumni affairs. Because alumni associations are expected to generate enough revenue to fully support their work on behalf of the university, there's a great need for alumni executives to look at their associations as for-profit businesses. But during our interview, James told me that in addition to the entrepreneurial spirit he brings to his work, it's his belief in connection that has ultimately kept all of his businesses profitable. "Connection builds trust—with your staff as well as with outside business partners. Without it, the organization will lose financially due to greater turnover and less external opportunities for new business."

In executive director positions at a variety of university-based alumni affairs offices, including the University of California, Irvine, James has consistently distinguished himself among his colleagues with his commitment to connection. I found it interesting to note that at the very beginning of our conversation, he appropriately noted that alumni associations exist to "create a lifelong connection between being a student and an active and supportive alumnus." It's a professional theme that also plays an important role in his approach to management.

Throughout his career, James has always brought his connections forward. That is, each time he was promoted or took on a new role in his career, he continued to build connections while benefiting from those already in existence. "For me, it's about more than networking. Connections generate revenue." As an example, James told me that he recently put together an event in London for UC alumni living in the United Kingdom. He said that several of the

> In my management style I encourage the importance of connections both inside and outside the university environment. I learned early on that the more connected you are in the workplace, especially in a university setting, the more successful you can be in getting high-quality work done more efficiently and even with less stress. I have also encouraged my employees everywhere I have worked to connect with business and corporate partners and appreciate the opportunities these relationships can bring. It's vital to anyone's career progression to always be building these connections.
>
> —James Stofan

companies who provided underwriting for the event were the result of connections he made early on his career. "Treating people in your network as partners in your work effort, and finding ways for the connection to benefit them as well, will bring rewards to you, your employees, and your organization. It all goes back to having trust and respect for those you meet and work with."

I had two questions for James as an out executive at one of the most gay-friendly educational institutions in the country. First, I wanted to know if he felt his commitment to the principle of connectivity had anything to do with his sexual orientation, and second, how working for an employer that provided a welcoming environment for gay employees had contributed to his approach to leadership. "I think the freedom you acquire from being out at work allows you to be successful at a higher level. Everyone has their own unique way of approaching situations and coming up with solutions, but if you're not able to draw on the real you to effect those solutions, you'll never be able to maximize your own potential." He continued, "Being gay has also given me a greater sensitivity to the needs of others, which has played a big part in being able to transform connections into solid and lasting business relationships—again, based on trust and respect. Real success is always rooted in these two credos."

Creating Tribal Knowledge

In *The Tipping Point*, Malcolm Gladwell identifies "connectors" as people who know everyone and unite others together.[2] They are the folks most responsible for the six degrees of separation theory, which asserts anyone can be connected to anyone else through a short chain of acquaintances—a maximum of five intermediaries. In G Quotient environments, gay executives empower their employees to become Gladwell-type connectors in addition to believing in the value of this behavior themselves. That old adage—the one about success being more about who you know than what you know—becomes less of an either/or proposition in G Quotient

> *Eighty-six percent of gay executives report that contacts with others in leadership roles frequently or always facilitate their success.*

environments and more of a successful dependency. In this sense, gay executives recognize that in their organizations (or tribes), connectivity generates knowledge, and therefore what you know often *depends* on who you know.

Because of the egalitarian nature of G Quotient environments, the final result of connectivity as a leadership principle involves the sharing of knowledge. When gay executives and their employees go out into the external world and connect with information, resources, and people to be more successful in their professional roles, what they find typically isn't kept proprietary unless security or legal reasons mandate privacy. Instead, it's openly shared in the tribe as a source for organizational success.

For the purposes of this discussion, *tribal knowledge* is defined as the collective, shared intelligence available to everyone in the organization or working unit. Tribal knowledge can therefore be used by anyone in the G Quotient environment for their own professional needs. I believe it's this precept that explains why 91 percent of employees reporting to gay managers said that communication between employees is encouraged in their workplace environment. Tribal knowledge is effective because when goals are shared, it's often the level of shared intelligence that keeps everyone moving in the same direction, and with greater purpose and efficiency. Tribal knowledge is therefore always in flux because as a result of connectivity, new intelligence will always flow in as well as being "walked in" by new employees' bringing their own set of unique intelligence.

By comparison, in pyramid-shaped hierarchies, tribal knowledge as it is defined here can never become an organizational success factor. Just as in that spider's web, it's the structure of G Quotient environments that facilitates the spreading of intelligence. When talking to both executives and their employees about this subject,

I also found that as intelligence spreads, there is an almost simultaneous process of interpretation, discussion, and at times disagreement over the validity and importance of the information. It's through this process that tribal knowledge becomes refined and formalized.

As communities of common interest, G Quotient environments use connectivity to leverage communication. Connectivity puts into place a twenty-first-century infrastructure that enables employees to instantly send and receive messages across the hall and across the globe. Being connected to information, resources, and people all over the world has unquestionably created brand new communication channels and behaviors. One of the most entertaining group exercises I do in my business communication class calls on students to share their favorite "emoticon" symbols as they define their digital communication style. This unique language didn't even exist two decades ago. Along with these new channels and behaviors, there is an accompanying need for a new type of organizational communication based on a new set of principles, as explored in the next chapter.

5

PRINCIPLE FIVE: COMMUNICATION

A friend of mine has a great newspaper cartoon taped to his office wall. In a world full of corporate misbehavior, the cartoon features two business titans talking about what they should do in light of all the recent ethical scandals dominating the news. The first one says, "We are seen as ethical disasters. How are we going to rebuild public trust?" The second one answers, "We could outsource it!"

In G Quotient environments, defining standards of ethical conduct begins with a commitment to authenticity and truth. As a principle of G Quotient leadership, communication represents an open system of verbal and nonverbal interaction between managers and employees committed to these same defining standards. Therefore, trust doesn't need to be outsourced, because the culture is consciously designed to manufacture it.

It's difficult to engage your employees if you communicate with them from a platform of false self-identity. In the case of gay executives, this of course has everything to do with being out of the closet in a friendly environment. Again, it's why closeted gay managers aren't identified as G Quotient leaders. But what's most important to understand is that, like all the other principles, this one applies to *every* manager regardless of sexual orientation. What it teaches is that if you're not using the strengths of your own individuality, it's impossible to acquire the type of credibility that's required for successful leadership in the recalibrated workplace.

Everyone wants to be heard, appreciated, and valued. At a time when employee engagement is inescapably tied to the affirming qualities of the workplace environment, communication in an organization becomes an even more complicated and emotionally charged process. Studies tell us that managers spend between 60 percent and 80 percent of their time involved in workplace communication.[1] In the Digital Age, with e-mail, instant messaging, BlackBerrys, and Palm Pilots, that entrenchment is not going away. Partly due to the difficulty of keeping secrets when private information is just a click away, authenticity and truth can no longer be considered merely positive qualities of a personality. They are indispensable leadership commitments that must guide all managers in how they communicate with their employees in the twenty-first century.

In practice, gay executives invite employees to see them for who they are as human beings while standing up for their own set of beliefs and principles. One of these beliefs is that it's impossible to successfully connect with your employees when you're living life in someone else's shoes. Why? Because it's difficult to convey a sense of personal value for your employees when you don't respect them enough to be real. What this means is that in its applied form, communication in G Quotient environments actively develops and nurtures interaction so as to create a culture that encourages and supports trust, facilitates organizational candor, and promotes cohesiveness.

Despite the pervasiveness of communication in the Digital Age and the distressed state of employee engagement across virtually all fields and industries, the call to build organizational communication systems that embody these three cultural properties is being ignored in far too many settings. I found that approaching leadership in one's own skin essentially predetermines the likelihood for gay executives to create these types of cultures, because authenticity and truth facilitate trust, which in turn helps both managers and employees in getting critical issues out on the table where they can deal with them—*together*. When you consider that 80 percent of employees reporting to gay managers stated that they trust their manager to advocate for their best interest in the organization, it becomes apparent that the correlation between authenticity and perceived trust is potentially significant.

Communicating with Authenticity and Truth:
Jarrett Barrios
State Senator (D), Massachusetts

Being out of the closet from the time he was sixteen made it impossible for Jarrett Barrios to become a closeted politician. The son of a carpenter and a social worker, Jarrett broke more than a few barriers when he entered Harvard at seventeen. Like other gay executives in my research, he has always been focused on what he believes is possible for himself, even if those possibilities conflict with what some in society term "traditional standards." During our interview he told me, "Going into politics was breaking all the rules, because I was gay *and* Latino."

After graduating with honors from both Harvard and then Georgetown Law School, he quickly established a premier reputation as a litigator before entering public life in 1998. Continuing to believe in all of life's possibilities, he ran for and was elected to the House of Representatives. Four years later, in 2002, he won the Massachusetts State Senate seat by a large majority in what began as a hotly contested primary election.

In this particular interview, I wanted to determine what set Jarrett apart from others who might have aspired to the same type of success but fallen short. I also wanted to know how that influenced his approach to leadership. Because Jarrett had to face and overcome the combined cultural barriers associated with his ethnic background as well as his sexual orientation, I believe his insight into this subject has particular significance. In his personal and public life, he has turned both minority affiliations into assets. What I found was a leader who understands the importance of communication based on authenticity and truth.

Jarrett told me that he believes a large part of his leadership role is to communicate the need for adopting new approaches to solving

Authentic communication invokes respect, which makes it a fundamental component of being persuasive. When the gay marriage debate was at its most intense here in Massachusetts, I made a speech about the value of my own family and the greater American value of equality. Almost immediately, I received over a thousand e-mails from people all over the country who had been watching my speech on television. What was most amazing was that the e-mails were primarily from straight people, who, even if they disagreed, said they appreciated the honesty of my message. I firmly believe that an appreciation for the truth can provide a platform for real and productive dialogue even on the most volatile of subjects. In politics, you are constantly being asked to identify your opposition and then go to work in an effort to turn them into proponents. It's a process that calls you to communicate with openness and a genuine commitment to your own beliefs.

—Senator Jarrett Barrios

problems faced by the people in his state. During our interview, he said that he often approaches communication in a way that will "clothe new ideas in traditional garb." It's a perfect example of how effective communication is best heard when there's a platform of mutual understanding. Developing successful political strategies in the Digital Age is not at all about trying to pull the wool over people's eyes. Instead, it's about using the truth to communicate why and how you can make a positive difference. "For me," Jarrett said, "it's about informing people that new ideas represent more than just a vehicle to protect the life and liberties they now enjoy. I believe that new ideas represent an opportunity to *improve* their quality of life."

As a profession, politics is one of those fields with a completely different landscape for doing business. "In politics," Jarrett told me, "today's enemies may be tomorrow's friends, by necessity." Jarrett's ability to maneuver what is arguably one of the most treacherous professions imaginable is deeply tied to a communication style that takes full advantage of *trust*. As a component of his leadership, it goes beyond how he communicates with his constituents and extends to how he communicates with his staff as well.

Like all politicians who have reached Jarrett's level of office, he's called upon to manage a campaign and legislative staff that includes a chief of staff, director of communications, legislative and budget director, and a director of administration. Being successful in a career field that he describes ultimately as being a "popularity contest," Jarrett has consistently communicated his own beliefs in a way that bridges, excites, and engages a broad spectrum of stakeholders including his employees. When I asked him to summarize the personal motivation that guides his career and his approach to leadership, he didn't need time to think about his answer. He simply said, "Doing well by doing good."

The Importance of Being Heard

Gay executives actively listen to their employees. As part of an open system of communication, active listening requires patience and respect for the speaker in addition to an acknowledgment of the message. Quite simply, empowered employees need to know they've been heard. Several gay executives told me that as a result of listening to their employees, they have significantly improved their response time in dealing with business problems and even internal conflicts, because they are brought into the communication loop early on. One executive told me that he always pays close attention to his employees because they're the ones in the trenches. He said, "If you want to find out what works and what doesn't work, for God's sake, ask the people doing the work!"

When managers take the time to actively listen to their employees and demonstrate an interest in what they are saying, they send a message of value. One gay executive told me that he views listening as a means to "validate the humanity of his employees." In cause-and-effect terminology, it partially explains why gay executives and their employees often form professional bonds rarely found in other working environments.

> *Ninety-four percent of gay executives report they frequently or always believe that successful management includes discerning the motivational pathways of their employees.*

As an interpersonal skill, listening is just as vital to the communication process as speaking. In G Quotient environments, actively listening to employees provided the following positive organizational effects:

- Increased professional bonds between managers and employees, because listening satisfies the employee's value need to be heard.
- Increased the truth factor in the environment, because active listening encourages direct communication between managers and employees with fewer third-party filters.
- Increases opportunities for managers to stay in touch with the processes of work in their organizations, preventing the ivory tower syndrome.

Because G Quotient environments have a much flatter playing field, there's less hesitation on the part of employees about communicating with their managers. As a practical benefit of communication, less hierarchy tends to enhance the speaking skills of employees and therefore make it easier for managers to be active listeners. Simply, there's less job title intimidation, the result being that messages are clearer, more concise, and—like the principle of communication itself—more open.

Leadership Heard Around the World:
Simon Bell
Director, A.T. Kearney

In his leadership role with the global management consulting firm A.T. Kearney—director of the firm's Global Business Policy Council—

Simon Bell is without question extremely well traveled. He facilitates business development and growth for clients all over the world. In just under two weeks, while we exchanged e-mail to set up this interview, he traveled to Hong Kong, Africa, the United Kingdom, Canada, and finally back to his home base in Washington, D.C. When we finally sat down to talk, I told him I had passport-envy.

All you have to do is spend a few minutes with Simon and you'll quickly understand how strongly he believes that authenticity, honesty, and effective leadership go hand in hand. Like other gay executives in my research, Simon clearly believes his approach to leadership is directly connected to having made the decision to come out in both his personal and professional life.

One of the more controversial subjects likely to come out of my research and this book relates to the fact that in terms of their approach to leadership, closeted gay men don't appear to have the same level of commitment to authenticity and truth that those who are out of the closet display. Because I found authenticity and truth to have a positive effect on employee engagement, job satisfaction, and workplace morale, it can be argued that closeted gay men are not succeeding as leaders to the same degree as their out-of-the-closet counterparts in the same four business sectors. Earlier research substantiates this logic, documenting that out-of-the-closet gays and lesbians who are employed in gay-friendly organizations earn 50 percent higher salaries than their closeted peers.[2] Simon offered this insight: "There's a watershed that happens between living in a false way and living in the truth. Over the course of my career, I've found the same positive dynamic that applies to one's personal life also applies to the workplace." When I asked him if he could explain how being out has influenced his approach to leadership, I seemed to strike a very positive chord. "For me, coming out was an amazing and liberating experience. Afterward, you discover that instead of the world falling down around you, things actually get much better. You get this 'ah-ha' realization that the truth is going to get you much further in life—and that includes your career."

People are smart and they can see through falsehoods. I give my employees a balanced and truthful viewpoint, and together we use that honesty as a foundation to move forward toward our goals. If you lead people in a certain direction based on falsehoods, you lose credibility and you're no longer a leader. That's why I trust in my own watershed and believe all good things will come from dealing with the world—and my employees—in a forthright way.

—Simon Bell

Among his employees, Simon told me, he's known for always giving a straightforward answer—even when that answer isn't exactly what people hoped to hear. In this respect, it's a behavioral example of how being heard facilitates organizational success. Being heard by today's empowered employees requires sending a truthful message. In the context of today's workforce, when leaders knowingly provide dishonest or disingenuous information to their employees, it not only becomes an insult to the individual as well as collective intelligence of the listeners, the dynamic between sender and receiver short-circuits. The result? Neither party "hears" the other from that point forward.

One of the great benefits I had in putting this book together was sharing my research connections with the leaders I interviewed. It created a wide-open dialogue, which often led me to discover some unanticipated insights into my own work. For example, when discussing the difference of opinion I found between gay male managers and straight male managers on the subject of how they feel about employees' moving on to new opportunities, Simon voiced some very strong feelings. "It's never made any sense to me when managers get upset or even angry when their employees are successful. Part of being a leader is acting as a mentor to your employees."

Among gay executives, I found a common belief that developing the potential of their employees is imperative for the short- and long-term success of their respective organizations. It's a belief reflected in my research. Ninety-two percent of gay executives reported that they frequently or always want to see their employees aspire to and attain higher positions. Simon continued on this sub-ject, "It's limited thinking to not look beyond the front door of your organization. I have contacts from Russia to India to Europe because employees have gone on to new opportunities. Even if someone chooses to look at this issue from a purely self-serving posi-tion, supporting your employees in their individual growth can only make you more successful."

Through his commitment to the career success of his own employees, Simon has engaged them as personal stakeholders in the organization and facilitated a greater level of trust between himself and his employees. Employees recognize and respect lead-ership when words and actions are aligned, and saying you care about an employee is validated when you participate in that employee's career success. It's another way to facilitate the neces-sary act of "hearing." As Simon already noted, what's important is the integrity of the communication. For contemporary employees, this type of authenticity and truth does more than breed trust; it communicates respect and value. It's the basis for being heard.

Communication and Ethics

As a force of influence within organizations, legal and ethical bound-aries play a pivotal role in how communication occurs in each envi-ronment. In business, legal and ethical boundaries provide the framework for communication to take place. Because local, state, and federal laws dictate how business can be conducted, we are legally restrained by these regulations. Ethics, on the other hand, are wide open for individual interpretation—even though they often provide even stricter boundaries and therefore have the potential to make a greater impact on organizational communication. While legal respon-sibilities provide the basic foundation, each person's individual belief system is what fleshes out the communication framework. As stated at the beginning of this chapter, ethical conduct in G Quotient envi-ronments begins with a commitment to authenticity and truth. Therefore, this same commitment guides the definition of ethics in determining what *quality* or *good behavior* actually is in these settings.

According to the 2004–2005 Workplace Forecast by the Society for Human Resource Management (SHRM), one of the greatest concerns HR professionals have is the "erosion of employee trust and organizational loyalty that ethics violations by company leaders can bring about." A secondary poll taken by SHRM along with the *Wall Street Journal's* CareerJournal.com, found that the perceptions employees have of the ethics of their organizational leadership may in fact be the biggest driver of employee trust and loyalty.[3]

When there is a divide between the ethical expectations leaders communicate for their employees and their own actions, all bets are off for empowered employees. Based on the parameters of legal and ethical boundaries, a combination of behaviors can take place—ranging from *illegal and unethical* to *legal yet unethical* to the best-case scenario, behavior that is both *legal and ethical*. One of the explanations for the extent of the erosion of employee trust is that ethics is simply not part of the dialogue in the majority of organizations. As ethics expert and communication professor Matthew W. Seeger of Wayne State University points out, "Managers are usually not trained to discuss ethics and often suffer from perceived powerlessness and general ambivalence with regard to ethical questions."[4]

Because of their open system of communication, G Quotient environments have a much broader and more truthful discourse that does include the subject of ethics. Therefore, employees have a much clearer understanding of how ethics is defined in these environments—as well as having the opportunity to actually influence and shape ethical meaning. Ultimately, it's about integrity and fairness, and bringing the organization together based on a common set of professional boundaries.

Keeping Everyone Honest:
Chad Spitler
Principal, Barclays Global Investors

A division of Barclays Bank, Barclays Global Investors (BGI) is one of the largest institutional money managers in the world—with more than $1.7 trillion in assets currently under its management. BGI is also a shareholder in most major corporations around the globe—and I'm not talking about owning minor interests. Chad Spitler, who is based at the company's offices in San Francisco, has the official job title of principal, corporate governance and proxy. In a post-Enron world, Chad's role has become even more important because it's his job to keep companies *honest*. As a shareholder, Barclays also has voting rights. So along with his team of analysts, Chad continually reviews and monitors how these companies are being run, interfacing with their CEOs and boards of directors on an ongoing basis.

Based on a statement delivered by the chairman of Barclays Bank at its annual general meeting in April 2005, it is clear that Barclays leadership believes profitable companies can and should benefit all stakeholders, including shareholders, customers, employees, and the community. Barclays disagrees with the point of view that the interests of these various stakeholders are incompatible. Many in the financial industry do believe that in order to maximize profits, it's acceptable to choose between shareholders and other stakeholders of the organization. Quoting from the chairman's statement, "We strongly believe that value is created, maximized, and sustained when the interests of all stakeholders are harmonized." This is a

Because it's my job to ensure that companies are communicating honestly about how their organizations are being managed, I am constantly made aware of how critical it is for leaders to approach the communication process as a two-way street. Effective communication is dependent on solid interpersonal relationships that are based on a foundation of honesty. It's impossible to guide or advise employees in the absence of truthful exchanges of information. In its truest sense, communication can't otherwise exist, because the messages going back and forth between the parties don't really exist if they don't represent the truth.

—Chad Spitler

belief that Chad brings to his work and approach to his own leadership every day.

Because Chad communicates with top corporate executives and boards of the world's largest companies, I asked if he approached these interactions differently from communications with his own employees. He said, "Other than being a more formal type of communication, it's still about effecting a truthful exchange. Otherwise I consider it blank communication, and everyone is wasting their time."

In his own organization, Chad told me, establishing an open system of communication means that he's able to create the type of bond between himself and his employees that, among other things, lends itself to having truthful exchanges. "From a problem-solving perspective, it's invaluable." He cited a recent example where several of his employees had gathered to talk about the stress they were experiencing in their working unit due to a particularly demanding schedule. Rather than just talking among themselves, they asked Chad to join in the discussion. "Because we've developed a culture where we respect each other's opinions and try to be as responsive as possible to each other's needs, they knew they could tell me the same thing they were telling each other. As a group, we were free to talk openly and honestly about how to solve these problems."

Open communication results in *direct* communication, and that makes for smoother problem solving. "There's just no room for hierarchal nonsense when your goal is to succeed as an organization," Chad told me. This is a belief that has repeatedly appeared throughout my research. Among employees who report to gay executives, 88 percent feel that they can disagree with their manager without fear of getting in trouble. Specifically, gay executives consistently told me they believe open and direct communication takes the venom out of the informal communication system that exists in so many workplace environments. Several remarked that in their own careers, they had previously worked in organizations where the negativity resulting from this type of informal communication system had all but shut down the processes of work.

The practical result from flattened, less hierarchal environ-ments is the reduced need for employees to create a separate system of communication to express concerns or discontent. Although informal communication systems still exist in G Quotient environ-ments, I found them to be focused mainly on social agendas rather than on outlets for anger or unhappiness.

I asked Chad, as someone who deals in honesty and truth, to share his thoughts on the connection between being gay and being an effective communicator. He immediately replied, "For me, there couldn't possibly have been a more difficult message to communi-cate than telling my parents that I was gay. I'm here to tell you that everything else pales in comparison." He continued, "When you come out you're really required to become a communication expert. You have to evaluate who people are and how they will likely take in and process what you have to say." Chad also told me he felt that when you grow up gay in a straight world, one of the ways you ini-tially adapt is to learn how to lie about who you are in the world. Today, he says, "I can spot a phony from a mile away, and I'm not talking about someone's sexual orientation. I know when someone is being less than honest, and in my job it's come in handy on more than one occasion."

I asked Chad how he communicates individual value to his employees. "For me it's about first having an appreciation for peo-ple's differences and then letting each person know that I value their contribution to the organization. Even just stopping in to say 'great job' to someone makes a tremendous impact." Going back to the formal and informal communication systems, Chad said, "You will never be invited into that informal network if you're not per-ceived as the kind of person who values and respects the contribu-tions of your employees."

Today's empowered employees have a great need to feel that they offer value to an organization. "No one responds in a positive way when they're made to feel that what they have to say isn't important. Even worse, if they're made to feel that it isn't smart. Once you devalue who someone is or discount their input, the communication link is severely damaged. In most cases there's no going back. That's why you have to get it right from the very beginning."

Communication in the Global Marketplace

Overall, I found that gay executives appear to have a distinct communication advantage when it comes to doing business as "global citizens" because of their belief in diversity as an organizational strength. As more and more U.S. businesses recognize the need to explore professional partnerships around the world, it's essential to this process to recognize that organizational communication must reflect an appreciative sensitivity and awareness of diverse cultural values. It's a process that prohibits the mind-set that other cultures should adhere to Western philosophies.

A secondary theme that emerged relative to this topic is the premium gay executives place on what can best be described as global consciousness. Already dominating European and Asian marketplaces, this is the belief that business can and should play a role in advancing humanity on a global level. In this sense, the importance of communication extends beyond the immediate workplace environment and into the global marketplace as a means to represent this new type of business ethos.

Henry David Thoreau, the American author and philosopher of the human condition, once said, "Speech is for the convenience of those who are hard of hearing; but there are many fine things which we cannot say if we have to shout."[5] In the context of the global marketplace, it will undoubtedly be the subtle language of respect that gives organizations the platform to communicate effectively around the world. Among the gay executives in my research, I found a widely held belief that expanding international markets depends on the aptitude of cross-cultural communication—particularly when it comes to matters of protocol, which requires not shouting but restrained dialogue. It also requires communicators to read between the lines, the subject of the next principle in the G Quotient paradigm.

6

PRINCIPLE SIX: INTUITION

As a principle of leadership, intuition is about gut instinct based on perceived truth, and it plays a positive role for G Quotient executives in organizational decision making from personnel matters to developing business relationships to committing to new deals and projects. Described earlier in this book as a "content filter" for thoughts and feelings that has historically enabled gay men to pick up on subtle or unspoken communication cues in order to distinguish between friend and foe, intuition relies on the collection of truthful information through *indirect* rather than direct senses. For gay executives, being attuned to these types of sensibilities in order to effect greater reasoning and processing of all types of business information is providing a leadership advantage across all four business sectors. Essentially, it translates into a heightened ability to perceive truth as individually defined.

Living in an age where ambiguity is mandated by constant change, many successful professionals "are turning to 'gut feelings' to assist them in creative problem solving and decision making."[1] In the workplace, relative to this particular leadership principle, it's fair to say that gay executives are capitalizing on this resource and blending traditional male power with traditional female insight with great business effects.[2]

Certainly history is full of stories about entrepreneurs who turned their intuition or gut instinct into major business successes. Since I'm from Southern California, the first one that comes to mind is Disneyland. When you look at the hard evidence, you wonder what criteria made Walt Disney believe that he could build a

> *Seventy-five percent of gay executives report frequently or always believing they are able to spot a good deal without necessarily hearing all the facts.*

theme park in an open field in what was then rural Orange County, California, and have people all over the world clamoring to get there? Based on cartoon characters, no less. In fact, it was only Walt, his brother Roy, and a handful of others who actually believed Disneyland would be successful. Walt once said, "I could never convince the financiers that Disneyland was feasible because dreams offer too little collateral." However, Disney's intuition told him that his idea would work, and he trusted his own perception of the truth—a move that now looks very sensible indeed.

In the fifty years since Disney called on his intuition to make one of the most successful decisions in his career, life has dramatically changed. With information coming at us 24/7, there is an accompanying need to develop new tools and skills to manage all that potential knowledge. In the case of intuition, it's not even *new* tools and skills, but simply tapping into age-old attributes of human consciousness that, for the most part, are widely underutilized in today's business landscape.

Intuition has long been a subject of interest among psychologists as a topic worthy of academic pursuit. John Dewey was arguably one of the most influential philosophers and educators of the twentieth century. He is recognized as one of the founders of Pragmatism, a school of philosophy characterized by the insistence that *truth* is defined by whatever contributes to the most human good over the longest course of time. Dewey's work on this subject is widely credited for stimulating the progressive movement in U.S. education during the first half of the twentieth century. In *Experience and Nature*, written in 1925, he stated that feelings have an efficiency that cannot be matched by thought. Dewey believed that even the most highly intellectual processes depend on feelings for guidance. "They give us our *sense* of rightness and wrongness, of what to select and emphasize and follow up, and what to drop, slur over and ignore among the multitude of inchoate meanings that are presenting themselves. . . . These qualities are the stuff of 'intuitions.'"[3]

Sexual orientation aside, as a strategy for effective leadership, *intuition* has a long way to go before it becomes a required course for business students. While it's more accepted and pursued as a business concept in professional circles outside the United States, intuition is still in its infancy of being understood as a *functional* ability. Why? Primarily because, as a tool for decision making, it's based on subjective rather than objective criteria. While few people would discount the role that intuition has played in the development of entrepreneur-run empires, the challenge in teaching intuition is pinpointing how this specialized type of intelligence comes into being. As a collective, gay executives demonstrate the ability to size up all constituencies relevant to their management roles and not just capitalize on their assets but also weed out undesirable influences.

More Than a Hunch:
Roland Jarquio
Manager, GE Consumer Finance

Roland Jarquio is brand strategy manager for the Americas at GE Consumer Finance. As the provider of financial services to both consumers and retailers in forty-seven countries with 110 million customers worldwide, the company has assets of over $151 billion. GE Consumer Finance, a unit of the General Electric Company, offers financial products that include everything from private label credit cards and auto loans to mortgages and credit insurance. To say it's a wide range would be an understatement. And it's Roland's job to develop overall brand strategy across multiple business units and countries.

With an MBA in management and strategy from Northwestern's Kellogg School of Management, Roland has unquestionably benefited from his own capacity to use intuition as a functional ability in his professional life. He started out as a consultant with the global strategy firm McKinsey & Company, where he advised senior-level executives from Fortune 500 companies on strategic decisions including growth and operations strategy. "Joining McKinsey first as a summer associate while still at Kellogg, and then making the transition into a full-time position as a consultant after graduation, proved to me that I had an intuitive talent where many of my colleagues struggled with something that just came naturally to me—reading people and situations."

During our first conversation, Roland told me that his ability to rely on his own interpretation of perceived truth became apparent during his junior year of college when he spent a year abroad in Caen, France. "It wasn't your typical study abroad program," he said. "This one required you to give up English for an entire year and to take classes among French university students as if you were one of them." Roland told me that being required to completely immerse himself in a foreign culture, even signing a contract stating that he would not speak English, focused his attention on the importance of being able to interpret those indirect communication cues and make decisions based on subjective criteria. "When you

I have relied on intuition starting with my first job as an usher at a movie theater at age sixteen. When I joined a consulting firm out of business school, I found that although many of my colleagues could devise elaborate solutions to complex problems, my natural ability to read people and situations gave me a distinct advantage. One recurring theme that came up in my performance reviews was my ability to get to the heart of a problem while conducting client interviews, and subsequently, being able to develop an effective strategy to address the problem. Another example would be how in my field of strategy consulting and marketing, I have often used intuition to develop consumer insights. I credit my intuition with giving me that something extra that allows me to see and hear more than other people.

—Roland Jarquio

can't communicate in your native language, you become very good at reading between the lines." It's an ability he has maximized throughout his career.

As a principle of leadership, intuition is more than just having a hunch. It's often about sensing energy levels in others, and, as Roland pointed out, having a ready comprehension of people and situations without needing a great deal of explicit detail. One of the most influential people to focus on this aspect of intuition was Carl Jung. Jung believed that intuition is one of the four types of functions that people use to take in information about the world they live in. In fact, Jung referred to intuition as "the ability to see around the corner."[4] In professional settings, gay executives use this ability to trigger creativity and explore solutions to problems that otherwise might have been overlooked. It's one of the reasons why Roland is successful at understanding and interpreting consumer needs. Intuition represents that "something extra" that gives him the heightened ability to recognize subtle and inherent truths in a variety of professional situations.

Among the gay executives in my research, I found a wide consensus that being able to capitalize on the principle of intuition requires a willingness to listen. On this subject, Roland told me that it wasn't until he came to terms with his own sexual orientation that he was able to focus the necessary level of attention on the external world in a way that actually allowed him to hear those subtle and inherent truths. "It's amazing how much energy is spent keeping the closet door closed. Until you're free of pretending to be someone else, you can't experience the type of awareness needed to see and hear other people and situations intuitively. You've got to read yourself before you can read others."

Defining Intuition as a Business Skill

To demystify this particular leadership principle a bit further, consider that *Webster's Dictionary* defines intuition as "quick and ready insight."[5] Everyone will agree that *quick* means fast, and *ready* means prepared. *Insight* refers to a clear or deep perception about people and situations. Therefore, intuition can alternatively be defined as being in a state of awareness that enables swift action.

What I believe can be understood from this simple string of definitions is that intuition isn't some type of mystical power. Instead, it clearly involves taking action based on both mental and physical preparedness. Thus it isn't something that is conjured; it's a knowledge-based process that allows people to discern the truth about realities that already exist. As a business skill, intuition is a product of the synergy created by the interaction of these simply defined terms. Going back to Walt Disney, when he settled on that open field fifty miles south of Los Angeles in the middle of nowhere, his intuition was based on an awareness that prepared him to make that landmark decision and influence our culture for generations.

As I stated earlier in this chapter, intuition is more widely embraced outside the United States. At Utrecht University in Amsterdam, one of the world's oldest universities (dating back to the seventh century), professor Fred Korthagen has developed an international reputation studying the impact of intuition. His work teaches that two important and complementary processes are associated with organizational learning—reflection and intuition. He describes reflection as "an important human activity in which people recapture their experience, think about it, mull it over, and evaluate it." He describes intuition as "seeing through things, getting down to what is implicit, uncovering the layer that lies beneath the surface."[6]

In this context, *reflection* most definitely addresses how awareness is developed. For gay executives, it's based on existing knowledge about information, facts, and ideas perceived as being truthful. In the United States, as holdover beliefs from the Industrial Age, reflection and intuition receive little attention in business leadership because these two concepts are still not viewed as having tangible value. It's a perfect example of the struggle many leaders are experiencing in giving value to intellectual capital. The prevailing mind-set holds that since intuition is not a machine that can be depreciated on a tax form, it has no commercial worth. Gay executives, on the other hand, approach intellectual capital from a very different viewpoint. For them, reflection and intuition do have commercial worth because each is seen as a knowledge-based behavior and therefore represents a new type of currency in the Digital Age.

Using Knowledge to Gain Intuition:
Tod Frank
Senior Project Manager, Quest Diagnostics

Quest Diagnostics is a company whose services you may have used without even knowing its name. As the leading provider of diagnostic medical testing, information, and services in the United States, it has clients that include patients and consumers in addition to physicians, hospitals, health insurers, employers, and government agencies. This Fortune 500 company performs personal health testing on more than 100 million patients every year. Now a senior project manager in Information Technology, Tod Frank has grown with the company since he joined it out of college almost twenty years ago. These days he devotes all of his time to the company's Nichols Institute in Orange County, California, where new tests and technologies are pioneered in the company's research and development efforts. For nearly two decades, Tod has had a front-row seat to witness how the Digital Age can transform an entire industry.

While technology has unquestionably revolutionized Tod's industry, one constant in his own professional life, throughout all the changes, has been his ability "to solve problems using every available resource at any given time." Tod told me that he considers his intuition to be a primary resource that has proven extremely useful throughout the technological transformation. As a mechanism for creating solutions, Tod noted, his intuition enhances his efforts to develop new and better technologies that ultimately serve to support the mission of his employer.

I use my professional intuition primarily for problem solving. I find that it allows me to leap to solutions with whatever information is available. Often, it's easier and faster to test a solution for viability rather than methodically create one. This is especially useful in the software development world, where problems that involve complicated programs escalate very quickly. On many occasions, we've been faced with software problems that required immediate debugging. My intuition not only saved us time but helped us prevent those already identified problems from growing larger.

—Tod Frank

Tod told me that he believes his ability to leap to solutions is an instinctive process that is a consequence of those truths he already knows. "I don't view my intuition as just coming out of thin air. It's based on my ability to quickly synthesize through information that I already possess in order to arrive at what I feel is a truthful judgment." When I asked Tod where he thought this ability comes from, he said, "It's definitely a process that has developed out of my own self-knowledge. If I didn't believe in who I am as a human being, I doubt whether I'd be able to recognize or trust my instincts relative to other people or situations."

In his hierarchy of needs theory, Abraham Maslow talked about how self-actualization is intrinsically tied to the human psyche. Because people tend to suppress their intuition and even creativity out of fear of knowing themselves too deeply, they also tend to avoid behaviors associated with these abilities. Gay executives have escaped this particular trap. Collectively, gay executives are confident in their ability, as Tod described it, "to quickly synthesize through information"—to take action based on already existing knowledge—without internal conflict.

Why? Maslow found that most people take the path of least resistance and conform to actions that fall within the status quo.

Simply put, it's easier and more comfortable. But gay executives are used to taking a less comfortable path as the result of not being on the Introduction's "moving sidewalk," so they are often willing to simply accept the truthful judgments emanating from intuition even if the resulting action may go against accepted norms. They can accept the intuitive process and its outcomes rather than avoiding or discounting their value.

Tod's ability to sense what other people are feeling also proved beneficial when he worked with HR to draft a new employment policy for the company that included sexual orientation, adopted in 1998. The following year, when he was named to the first corporate Diversity Leadership Team and subsequently co-founded the company's first officially sanctioned LGBT employee resource group, he once again found that trusting his intuition enhanced his interpersonal communication and contributed to his ability to make a positive impact on organizational culture.

I thought Tod, being a technology expert, would be the perfect person to ask if it's possible to summarize his own intuitive methodology. After thinking about it for a moment, he said, "Intuition requires you to look at the entire picture without having your perception blocked by bias or fear of what your intuition may reveal. To do that, you have to first trust in your own mental database of knowledge, because that's where intuition comes from. Ultimately, you have to trust in yourself."

> I find that I get a quick sense of what people are feeling about the subject at hand, regardless of their words. I tap into this ability in all types of work-related communication by trusting what my intuition is telling me about a person or a situation. It's my goal as a manager to create an environment where people feel secure enough to trust in their own intuition as a way to problem solve and create solutions.
>
> —Tod Frank

Tapping into Perceptual Intelligence

To a large degree, the intuitive process in G Quotient environments depends on the level of perceptual intelligence of the person using intuition as a business skill. Because the context of virtually all industries is constantly subject to change, organizational leaders are now in a position to augment and reorganize their perceptions about their industries, organizations, and employees on an ongoing basis. Without this type of mental restructuring, sustaining success over time will prove impossible, because so much of organizational reality is consistently new and therefore previously unknown in the environment.

Howard Gardner, professor of cognition and education at Harvard, says, "When you're entering an area where the unknowns are high, and experience is important, if you don't rely on intuition you're cutting yourself short."[7] Overload has become part of organizational life. Unknowns are virtually immeasurable, and analytical, left-brain logic can only partially address today's demand for leaders to always be ready to take quick and accurate action. To meet this demand, leaders are continually obliged to acquire new perceptual intelligence. To do so requires an open mind along with a commitment to observing people and their environments, and, of course, how they relate to each other. Collectively, gay executives nurture and further develop their intuition because they are conditioned to scan their environment and its inhabitants, synthesize these new perceptions, and trust in their findings as a basis for making decisions and taking action.

Perceptual intelligence as a basis for intuition is highly relational between both left- and right-brain processes. The terms *right brain* and *left brain* are so ingrained in our culture that it's sometimes easy to forget what they mean and that the research behind them was quite revolutionary. The discovery that human beings are of two minds was made by Roger Sperry, a psychobiologist whose research found that the brain operates in two distinct ways—with its hemispheres in harmony as well as independent of each other.

Sperry, who won the Nobel Prize in 1981, did groundbreaking work in the early 1960s on *split-brain* individuals—those where the connection between brain hemispheres had been severed—which indicated that certain abilities were focused in one part of the brain as opposed to the other. He found that the left hemisphere of the brain tended to function by processing information in analytical, rational, and sequential ways. He also determined that the right hemisphere perceives in images and feelings.

Because intuition is primarily a right-brain process, it's easy to see why conservative corporate environments dominated by straight white males have historically shied away from intuition as a principle of leadership. According to the societal stigma, right-brain processes deal with unscientific or illogical reasoning and, traditionally speaking, are considered to be more feminine and therefore weaker. To attach any organizational value to intuition would be a threat to the identity of most Industrial Age paradigms.

However, perceptual intelligence as a resource for intuition relies on the combined use of right- and left-brain functions. It's about seeing details and facts as well as taking in the big picture, which includes images, emotions, and imagination. Therefore, while intuition is characterized as a type of rapid insight, it's often supported by extensive logic and reasoning. Because of the ever-changing business, political, and societal landscape, categorizing intuition as either masculine or feminine is no longer valid—it's a matter of utility as opposed to gender.

Acknowledging and developing intuition as a business skill not only provides sound and truthful criteria to make decisions, it leads to the ability, as Roland has experienced, to "read between the lines." As a criterion for making truthful assessments about people and situations, it also contributes to immediate solutions and problem solving, as Tod described. In the twenty-first century, intuition can and should play an important role in how leaders meet organizational challenges. Intuition is a tool—a business skill and not an intangible weakness—that creates a competitive advantage in a world that presents leaders with a myriad of organizational choices on a daily basis.

Albert Einstein once said, "The only real valuable thing is intuition." In G Quotient environments, the value of intuition is considerable, contributing to enlightened leadership on a variety of levels from creativity and innovation to interpersonal communication. In all four sectors, I found that gay executives collectively embrace the influence of their surroundings in order to scan internal knowledge as well as external environments. As a mechanism to aid in the accomplishment of professional goals and objectives, intuition ultimately represents the opportunity for instant organizational comprehension.

7

PRINCIPLE SEVEN: COLLABORATION

Each year *Fortune* and the Hay Group identify the most admired companies in the United States and around the world. They also identify the business practices that contribute to each company's success. In 2005, they found that the most admired companies "distinguish themselves from others by fostering cultures that support collaboration."[1] In G Quotient environments, gay executives view themselves as builders of organizational cultures where collaboration is believed to contribute to the conceptual and physical processes relative to the development and management of their organizations. Thus the principle of collaboration represents much more than simply teamwork in these environments.

As the final principle of G Quotient leadership, collaboration depends upon and grows out of the practice of each of the first six principles. Without inclusion, creativity, adaptability, connectivity, communication, and intuition, collaboration will always struggle to exist. Why? Because collaboration requires a new ethos of leadership that fully capitalizes on the potential of today's empowered employees.

In G Quotient environments, this expanded meaning of collaboration impacts what I define as the three organizational P's: planning, proficiency, and profitability. Each represents a function of organizational success that is realized through maximizing employee potential. The first of the three functions, *planning*, begins with placing the right resources in the workplace environment and then linking individual employees to them appropriately. It's the first step gay executives take in building a culture designed to make the most

> *Eighty-seven percent of gay executives frequently or always depend upon their employees for new ways of accomplishing tasks and meeting goals.*

of all its resources. Planning therefore provides the functional context for employees to do excellent work and is designed to prevent isolation as well as foster a culture where success is recognized as being an outcome of the entire organizational system.

As a result of planning, accomplishment becomes possible because it places the organization in a position to achieve the second P, *proficiency*. In G Quotient environments, employee potential is maximized because people are widely in roles that take advantage of their talents and skills as well as facilitating their professional growth. In this sense, collaboration develops the intellectual (knowledge) capital of the organization. Last in the three P's is *profitability*, which is viewed as stemming from planning and proficiency. It's why the principle of collaboration anchors the G Quotient paradigm, it provides ongoing economic viability.

Collaboration rather than supremacy represents a necessary condition for organizational achievement. Across all four sectors, I found that gay executives believe in sharing authority. Their approach reflects the new type of power discussed later in this book. Like inclusion, the principle of collaboration requires leaders to demonstrate respect and value for their employees. Respect and value act as catalysts for collaboration, bringing the G Quotient paradigm full circle. In G Quotient environments, collaboration contributes to engagement and satisfaction because it contributes to the equilibrium of the organization as a system.

When organizations are built on pyramid-shaped hierarchies, employees are less likely to venture outside their zone of familiarity and collaborate with others. Hierarchal structures encourage employees to grab the glory for themselves because that's how success has traditionally been defined and rewarded. Today, this reward system is completely out of balance with the new world of work.

Conversely, G Quotient environments are structured to support and reward collaboration. There's an old business philosophy that says how things get recognized in the organization will subsequently become the modus operandi for getting things done. Meaning, collaboration will have value if it is recognized and rewarded in the organization. Among the gay executives in my research, both are built-in consequences of this final leadership principle.

Maximizing Employee Talents:
Trevor Burgess
Executive Director, Morgan Stanley

Trevor Burgess is an investment banker at Morgan Stanley in New York City. As executive director for global capital markets, he manages teams of investment bankers all around the world, each responsible for raising equity and debt capital for a wide variety of companies across industry sectors. This is a key role at one of the country's leading financial institutions: Trevor puts together and executes hundred-million-plus and even billion-dollar transactions including IPOs from New York to Brazil. When we spoke, his current management portfolio included eight teams of investment bankers across the globe working on corporate finance transactions.

One of the things that impressed me most about Trevor was how accessible and down-to-earth he is for someone who deals in billions of dollars on a daily basis. As an organizational leader, his belief in the value of professional community is completely genuine. What really matters, Trevor said, is "getting the best people together and being open to the possibilities that they bring to the table."

Like the majority of other gay executives I interviewed, Trevor told me that he doesn't care if it's him or a member of his team who has the best idea. "Ego," he said, "cannot play a role in how you make profitable decisions." When I asked him if he thought there was a connection between being gay and being able to keep ego out of the decision-making process, he brought up an intriguing point.

A culture of collaboration leads to a culture of excellence. My goal as a leader is to become a trusted adviser to all of my employees and my clients. To do so, you have to first develop a reputation for being someone who believes that success is team-based and not leader-based. Once people recognize that you value their opinions and respect their desire to be heard as professionals, you gain their trust. Without collaboration, the best that everyone has to offer will never be brought forward to help serve our clients.

—Trevor Burgess

"It reminds me of that cliché complaint women have about their boyfriends or husbands refusing to stop and ask for directions. For myself, I don't view asking for advice as being an affront to my masculinity. In fact, I see it as a strength. You can't let your ego become a barrier between you and arriving at the best possible outcome for a client."

Trevor told me that he continually looks for ways his teams can do more than just reach their final destination. "It's my goal for us to always beat client expectations once we get there." In this sense, he said, it's vital for everyone to get on board with the belief that working as a team is necessary for organizational success as well as being clear about their individual team roles. As builders of organizational cultures where collaboration facilitates the processes of work, gay executives believe it's necessary for their employees to understand both the importance of their role and the way it contributes to organizational achievement. "From planning to execution, collaboration is *how* my organization effects success."

Successful collaboration requires dependability and reliability. On this subject, Trevor said, "There must be an unparalleled commitment to excellence in our organization. Being 'off' 1 percent is unacceptable when you're talking about a billion dollars. When people understand how important they are as members of the team and that their work is needed and valued, that commitment almost always follows." As a believer in true meritocracy, Trevor also sees collaboration playing a role in how people get ahead based on their abilities. "Protecting information rather than sharing it is an old way to succeed. I want transparency in my organization, because in order to work as a team toward a shared client outcome, there has to be shared information. Collaboration can't occur when there's separation."

I asked if Trevor felt collaboration played a bigger role in his approach to leadership than it does for peers at other companies. Pausing for a moment, he said, "Because I think gay men are more apt to judge people based on the content of their character rather than demographics, there's a climate created within the organization that's conducive to collaboration. When we reach a certain level of success, I think collaboration plays a larger role in how we manage. It also has a great deal to do with fairness, meritocracy, and giving everyone a chance to participate."

As part of his leadership, Trevor told me, he pays a great deal of attention to how people view themselves. Trevor feels that understanding how individual members define their own professional value is necessary for him to maximize the organizational benefits of a team-based environment. "Beyond assembling the best possible minds to work together in my organization, I want people to develop their expertise in a way that's meaningful to them. Finding out what matters to people and where they want to go helps me put together more effective teams. It also makes their work more meaningful, which, at the end of the day, contributes to our team's standing apart from the crowd."

Creating Professional Community

The 2005 report by Hay Insight of 1.2 million employees in more than four hundred organizations worldwide found that less than half (49 percent) stated that their company had a generally cooperative atmosphere.[2] Mark Royal, a senior consultant with Hay Insight, said that it was a lack of cross-functional teamwork in these environments that led to "lower levels of productivity and growth and makes it much more difficult for organizations to operate efficiently or achieve their strategic objectives."

In G Quotient environments, gay executives promote cross-functional teamwork by capitalizing on the value of professional community as a means to create organizations that are more welcoming, affirming, and balanced. Broadly defined, professional community can describe any group of individuals who share common professional interests and goals. The utility of professional community is unquestionably based on the business merits of mutual exchange. Specifically, in G Quotient environments, I found that gay executives build professional community around the intellectual capital of their employees. This accounts for why professional community (in the context of the leadership principle of collaboration) is as much about individual employees as it is about the group. Because the value of professional community is based on the talents, skills, and unique needs and goals of each employee, it's constructed to facilitate individual success through the group or community effort.

Because G Quotient environments are built around the idea that boundaries hinder collaboration, gay executives believe that if you are stuck in a box or ring, you are unable to link with the intellectual capital of others in the organization. Collaboration also makes for a happier workplace because it connects people to one another as human beings. It's one of the reasons why, as cited in the Introduction, 84 percent of employees reporting to gay managers state that morale in their working units is high.

Creating Community:
Kevin Colaner
Executive Director, Admission and Academic Services, USC Rossier School of Education

As at many large universities, several academic schools make up USC. At the Rossier School of Education, the focus is decidedly on molding educational leaders rather than simply preparing teachers.

> Leadership is about building collaborative and positive work communities. I approach my role with a belief that it's not all about me. It's my job to facilitate success for every one of my employees. One of my guiding principles has always been to leave an organization in better shape than I found it. That can't happen without developing a team-based culture that has meaning for everyone involved. Collaboration requires cooperation and trust at all levels, and the best way to get there is to give your employees what they need to succeed.
>
> —Kevin Colaner

As executive director of the Office of Admission and Academic Services, Kevin Colaner is responsible for making sure the students entering the school's programs are competitive, driven, and a good fit with the university.

One of the most memorable take-aways for me on this particular interview was the clear commitment Kevin has made in his leadership role in creating a collaborative workplace system. As with other gay executives, it's his systems approach to management that has directly contributed to an emphasis on teamwork in his organization. "Early in my career I would try not to be bothered if an employee seemed out of sorts or disconnected. But for me that wasn't a truthful response. I do care if someone is unhappy in my organization, because it's my responsibility to make sure working here is a positive experience for everyone. In that sense, I believe managers *should* take it personally."

Having worked in organizations earlier in his career where he wasn't out of the closet, Kevin believes he's a better leader today than when he was closeted in his professional life. "Speaking from firsthand experience, the process of 'coming out' made me a more effective manager, because I've lived in that place where it's not OK to be yourself. It gave me such an appreciation for everyone's diversity—and I don't just mean that in terms of ethnicity or sexual orientation—but whatever defines you as a human being. In that sense, I strive to create an environment where everyone can come out."

In G Quotient environments, the principle of collaboration represents the constant opportunity to engage employees in the processes of work. In Kevin's case, it's been a management tool that he's used with excellent results in several different environments. "Several times in my career, I've found myself taking on a new role that requires me to turn an organization around from the effects of what could best be described as autocratic management. I believe this is one of my personal strengths—creating a new culture in environments where employee morale is in serious trouble." When I asked him why, he said, "I suppose part of it is tied to the feeling that I have to work harder and be more effective because I'm gay. The other part is that I truly enjoy making things *right*. It's a terrible injustice to be treated unfairly at work. I get a great sense of accomplishment when I can make work better for a group of people who haven't had the opportunity to excel at what they do."

How does he approach a turnaround? "The first thing I do is put a new game plan in place that gets everyone involved in a meaningful way. One of the best ways I've found to develop a team-based environment and restore morale is to return the responsibility of work to the employees. The knowledge and confidence that people gain when they're given a chance to do their job—without the fear of getting blamed should something go wrong—is transformational. I believe good leadership is about getting an organization to a place where your employees say, 'I'm planning on doing this, what advice can you offer,' as opposed to 'Can I do this?'"

Proficiency, defined earlier in this chapter as one of the three organizational "P's," is one consequence of the type of job ownership that Kevin has found to play a key role in making over a workplace environment. When people have some autonomy over their job, they get good at it. At one point during our interview, Kevin said, "I don't understand how managers can expect their employees to grow if they don't give them the chance to exercise their professional know-how. If you're never allowed to act on your own ability, which includes decision making, by the way, how can the job truly be yours?"

Many employees in G Quotient environments use the word *family* to describe their feelings about their workplace. When I asked Kevin how he feels when an employee decides to move on, he didn't hesitate, "It's great," he said. "In fact it's one of the best compliments I can receive as a manager. When someone who works for me goes on to bigger and better things it means I've done my job." The environment he creates is so good, in fact, that people often feel bad about leaving—something I heard repeatedly among both G Quotient leaders and their employees. Kevin sums up that point nicely: "Having an employee tell me that he or she wants to take their career to the next step, but doesn't want to leave the environment I've helped create, is something I believe every manager should aspire to. When someone leaves, we have a party, get sentimental, and send them on to their next career step with what is hopefully a set of experiences that will add to their success."

Collaboration and Self-Disclosure

In all types of relationships, professional or personal, self-disclosure is necessary for developing trust. I found that in G Quotient environments self-disclosure plays a primary role in how gay executives create a culture where employees can enjoy the security to become full participants in the collective team or group. *Webster's Dictionary* defines *trust* as the "assured reliance on the character, ability, strength, or truth of someone or something."[3] Therefore, it can be argued that trust is primarily based on perception. In this sense, "assured reliance" is completely dependent on the observations, senses, as well as individual or group vantage point of employees.

Beyond the value of sharing information about one's life away from the organization so as to humanize the manager-employee relationship, professional self-disclosure also includes honest feedback about the conceptual and physical processes of the organization. And it isn't limited to feedback delivered solely to employees.

One executive summed this sentiment up by telling me, "The last thing I want is a bunch of bobble-heads shaking their heads in affirmation of everything I say. That's not collaboration, that's a monarchy." It's a great illustration of this communication dynamic: successful relationships can occur only if there is a balance between self-disclosure and feedback. Making information known to both parties is imperative to building a collaborative environment because it contributes to those perceptions of assured reliance on which trust is born.

Noted scholars of gender issues have found that gay men are more likely to self-disclose and to be better at it than straight men, because they don't buy into the "strong silent type" as a behavior model. Thus gay men are more at ease when called on to communicate their thoughts and feelings.[4] When I brought this theory up to several of the executives interviewed for this book, I found general agreement tempered with an important qualification. Self-disclosure, I was told, isn't about "endless chit-chat," nor is it about telling someone your entire life story at a staff meeting. There was a definite progression to the level of self-disclosure that occurred over time. Based on these parameters, the connection between gay executives and their employees strengthened over time—as noted, to the point that many employees in these environments are reluctant to leave. Ultimately, in G Quotient environments, collaboration creates tremendous individual meaning.

Orchestrating a Collaborative Environment: Mike Syers
Partner, Ernst & Young

As a partner in E&Y's Transaction Advisory Services division, Mike Syers heads up the firm's New York–based team of partners, consultants, and staff specializing in mergers and acquisitions in the real estate and hospitality industry. He is also one of the partners leading a growing national practice of more than a hundred professionals in ten offices. Transaction Advisory Services, or TAS as it's known in the field, is one of E&Y's fastest-growing practices, helping clients make the best possible business decisions to "maximize opportunity while minimizing risk." In addition to having management responsibility, Mike is also a client-serving partner—meaning that he's always in the trenches doing everything from working with clients and running teams to signing off on projects and billing for professional services.

Prior to joining the firm as a direct admit partner in 2002, Mike was a partner at Arthur Andersen when today's Big Four accounting firms was still the Big Five. To understand the effectiveness of Mike's leadership and his commitment to collaboration, it's important to understand how he and his team got to E&Y. When Arthur Andersen found itself in the middle of the Enron scandal, Andersen employees began to splinter off all around the country. Under Mike's leadership, his practice at Andersen was widely recognized in the field as being highly ethical, successfully managed, and profitable—which is why E&Y decided to import Mike's complete business unit into its own firm in 2002. The stature of the practice also led other companies to attempt to hire away many of Mike's employees before negotiations with E&Y even began. But while other Andersen employees were quickly breaking away, Mike's team refused to separate. They wanted to stay together as a team, almost unheard-of, considering the circumstances.

Mike's commitment to creating an environment where collaboration is achieved through honesty and respect generated the type of loyalty among his employees that ultimately sustained his team through a very difficult time. At the end of the storm, they emerged as a fully engaged and productive team in a brand new professional home. Several years later, thanks to E&Y's belief in putting people first and supporting a diverse and inclusive workforce, Mike is even more convinced that collaboration leads to organizational success.

From a leadership perspective, collaboration is about turning individual movement into team movement, and then turning team movement into organizational movement. As Mike pointed out, collaboration begins with employees being able to "bring themselves fully to the workplace." I asked Mike how he turns this goal

Collaboration is orchestrated. It begins with creating an environment where employees are able to bring themselves fully to the workplace. It's impossible to have a team-oriented culture unless everyone feels welcome. Putting people first allows me to find out who my employees are as individuals so I can then recognize how they will best fit and work within the group. To be an effective leader it's necessary to tap into the professional needs and values of your employees, and that requires honesty and respect. Once that's accomplished, the igniting spark that makes it all come together is trust. It's the final ingredient for any leader seeking to cultivate a collaborative organization.

—Mike Syers

into a reality. "Employees have to feel their manager is approachable as a person, and not just an authoritarian figure who is constantly judging them. Being able to relate to your employees as a person rather than a boss is one of the how-to actions that brings about collaboration in any organization."

"People have lots of interests outside the workplace," Mike said, "and taking the time to learn about the interests of my employees, as well as sharing my own, nourishes the trust level within the organization." Further, Mike said, he believes this type of exchange "creates a more balanced perception of who each other is in the world. It creates trust, and in order to trust someone you have to know them. It's why great teams are so effective." Mike told me that he has always believed in telling his employees the truth and not giving them a company line, and that this helped his team remain together and weather the Andersen storm effectively. "My employees trusted me to tell them the truth about what was going on during that entire time. It's one of the reasons why we never stopped being productive. The act of honest disclosure kept us from becoming isolated from each other, which allowed us to continue to successfully serve our clients."

When Mike started his career in the mid-1980s, he didn't think he had a long-term career opportunity working for the big accounting firms. "I had pretty much completed the process of coming out in my personal life, but in the big firms, there weren't visible gays or lesbians in leadership positions. After working so hard to get honest in my personal relationships with family and friends, I knew I didn't want to spend energy at work trying to be someone other than myself." Essentially, it was his own belief in being able to bring himself fully to the workplace that strengthened his commitment to this principle as a manager.

When Mike became a partner at Ernst & Young, the first big accounting firm to score 100 percent on HRC's corporate equality index, he found a "meeting of the minds" about the belief that people have to come first. "It wasn't a case of having to go against the grain of the firm to be the kind of leader I wanted to be. The level of acceptance that I've felt as an employee myself at E&Y has given me the opportunity to experience the same positive benefits that I've always tried to provide my employees." In fact, just a few weeks prior to our interview, Mike "came out" to three thousand partners at Ernst & Young's partner meeting in Orlando, Florida. "If you had told me twenty years ago that I would be sharing my personal story in a video segment about how one of the big accounting firms is committed to creating an inclusive environment where all employees are equally valued as people, I never would have believed you."

Admittedly, Mike was a little nervous about reaction to the video. Describing himself as a private person by nature, going before the camera and sharing himself with organizational peers from all over the country was a bit daunting. But it was also about something he has known all along: "To trust someone, you have to know them." As soon as the video ended, while he was still seated in the enormous conference center, Mike's BlackBerry began to go off. The messages said "great job" and "keep up the good work." Several read, "I'm so proud of you and our firm!" What he wasn't expecting was how many straight partners came out as friends and allies, sharing with him their own personal stories about their gay and lesbian children, brothers, sisters, and friends. Describing this experience, Mike said, "It was most definitely about that final ingredient of trust. It's the glue that holds an organization together as a team and makes collaboration a reality."

Part Two

G QUOTIENT LEADERSHIP IS BUILT TO LAST

G Quotient leadership changes lives. For the people who work in these environments, G Quotient leadership has contributed to the enrichment of their families, instilled individual confidence, developed self-esteem, and opened up their worldviews in a way that has changed their hearts and minds. For anyone who still subscribes to the philosophy that employees should leave their personal lives at the organizational doorstep, I simply suggest that it's time to find out why this compartmentalized type of thinking has become obsolete. Accordingly, the next section of this book focuses on why the G Quotient is built to last.

In a globally connected world, the actions of management indeed have the promise of making a negative or positive impact on society through their impact on employees. And the seven G Quotient principles presented in Part One have contributed to a better quality of life in very personal ways for employees in these environments.

Thinking beyond the next ten years in terms of what will define successful business leadership is a bit like trying to forecast political elections. You never know what new discovery or unexpected development might surface to change the course of history. However, while it's true no one can predict what changes lie ahead, even in the immediate future, nonetheless certain clear and identified trends will continue to influence the needs and values of tomorrow's employees.

To detail why gay executives are winning the leadership race, this book has explored the reconstruction of contemporary employees along with the development and refining of the fundamental learned skills of gay men (adaptability, intuitive communication, and creative problem solving). Combined with the social, historical, and political context of our time, all these factors have converged to set the stage for the success of a new type of business leadership. All these influences focus primarily on where we have been and where we are now. And, while I personally believe it's precarious to make definitive predictions about criteria for successful leadership beyond the next ten years, I'm comfortable in stating that many of the underlying reasons that have already contributed to the evolution and success of G Quotient leadership will be further evidenced in the immediate future.

8

WHY G QUOTIENT
LEADERSHIP WORKS

The new workplace playing field became glaringly evident to me in 2003, during a lunch with recruiting executives from General Mills at the University of Southern California. With annual revenue that exceeds $10 billion, General Mills was in the process of selecting our university as a primary recruiting source on the West Coast. I, along with several seasoned business professors and administrators, had been invited to share our perspectives about the career expectations and workplace values that define Gen Y college graduates. Like executives in many successful organizations, the executives from General Mills expressed concern about recruiting new talent amid declining national statistics of employee engagement—illustrated most significantly by depressed rates of job satisfaction and workplace morale. They also discussed the financially troubling issue of employee turnover, which of course factored into General Mills's recruiting strategy: hire new talent that they hoped would stay longer than a year or two before moving on to other opportunities.

As you might imagine with a group of business scholars, the conversation soon turned to research and percentages. Polls conducted by some of the largest and most respected information companies in the world were starting to bring alarming news. Consider that over a span of time ranging from the mid-1990s to the present, the downward trend in employee engagement statistics has taken a giant-size toll on the state of this nation's workplaces. For example, according to the *Gallup Management Journal*, 71 percent of U.S. employees are either disengaged or actively disengaged from their work.[1] In terms of job satisfaction, The Conference Board, one of the world's most influential business organizations and dedicated to the state of the global marketplace, found that job satisfaction has declined across all income brackets in the last nine years—the largest decline being among workers between the ages of thirty-five and fifty-five, falling to just under 50 percent.[2] (And these observations continue to this day. For example, Towers Perrin, in the largest single study of the workforce on a global basis, announced in November 2005 that in the United States, only 21 percent of workers are fully engaged. According to the Towers Perrin study, "U.S. employees remain frustrated and skeptical about both their senior leadership and how well their company is delivering on their 'employment deal.'"[3] In the latter part of 2005, an Accenture study found that middle managers in the United States are increasingly dissatisfied with how their companies are being managed, with fewer than half [48 percent] feeling positive about their own employers. (This represents a decline of nearly 20 percent over the same survey just one year earlier.[4]) Regardless of which poll you believe to be more accurate, the bottom line is that employee engagement, job satisfaction, and workplace morale among U.S. employees was in bad shape in 2003 and is now reaching critical levels.

Many of my colleagues around the table at the General Mills lunch had benefited from being in the trenches through both generations X and Y. My own vantage point as a university lecturer was enhanced by having had the privilege as an administrator to meet and get to know recruiting managers from organizations all over the world. Being in the unique position to hear unfiltered perspectives from both students and employers, I have often felt like the proverbial middle man, negotiating between what can only be described as widely disparate expectations.

As our conversation segued from the career expectations of new graduates to those of more experienced employees, including ourselves, it became apparent that professional excellence can no longer be achieved without an authentic sense of both personal connection and meaning. Immediately after the General Mills lunch, I went back to my office and quickly added a question to a survey tool I was about to send out to hiring managers throughout the Fortune 500. "Do you believe that feeling valued as an individual by your supervisor is going to be more or less important to employee engagement over the next ten years?" The answer turned out to be an overwhelming *More*. Ninety-three percent of respondents weighed in with "more important."

Since 2000, student voices on the subject of employee needs have become equally loud. Big-name companies with reputations for autocratic leadership, once inundated with résumés because of their name-brand prestige, are being widely ignored as potential employers. The bottom-line message we delivered to our friends at General Mills was right on target. The next generation of professionals would not respond favorably to leadership that even hinted at Industrial Age power structures. As it turns out, our message didn't just apply to the needs and expectations of graduating college students; it also addressed the needs and expectations of seasoned professionals at all career levels.

It's a Brand New Neighborhood

The 2000 U.S. census should have been a wake-up call to any manager still trying to apply old leadership paradigms to today's workforce. In addition to individual empowerment being a driving force behind the reconstruction of contemporary employees, cultural diversity has forever changed the world of work as well as the consumer marketplace. In the United States, between 1990 and 2000, the foreign-born population nearly doubled, to 31 million. Saul Gitlin, executive vice president for strategic services at Kang & Lee Advertising, a division of Young & Rubicam, estimates that the total size of the Asian, Hispanic, and African American population in the United States is equal to the entire baby-boomer generation. In 2004, among the companies that made Diversity Inc.'s list of top fifty companies, nearly half of their promotion budgets targeted multicultural markets.[5]

As part of the new workplace neighborhood, many organizations are hiring high-level executives dedicated to capitalizing upon, managing, and leveraging corporate diversity to strengthen their organizations. To understand the importance of these positions, all you have to do is follow the money. Ranging from directors to vice presidents to chief officers, these positions offer very high salaries and carry a great deal of clout. In fact, 92 percent of CEOs report that they personally review the diversity metrics within their organizations on a continual basis.[6]

Based on a Diversity Best Practices survey of 179 of the 500 largest U.S. companies, the following facts detail—in dollars and more dollars—the organizational importance of diversity:

- *Average annual salary of diversity executive:* $225,000
- *Average department budget:* $2.8 million (estimated 2006)
- *Department size:* An average of 8.2 internal staff with approximately 30 percent of companies allocating 21 people or more to this function
- *Average tenure:* Ten years at the company; four years in the position

In homogenous environments, new ideas can easily go untested or unchallenged because everyone thinks the same way based on the same set of life experiences—even at the board of directors level. A 2003 study examining the relationship between board diversity and firm value among Fortune 1000 companies presented empirical evidence of a significant and positive correlation between board diversity and improved financial value.[7] For several decades, researchers in the social sciences have studied not just the functioning but actual flourishing of those urban settings where diversity adds to the effectiveness of how communities interact through a multitude of networks. Diverse environments, whether organizational or regional, significantly contribute to the economic well-being of both settings partly due to much greater levels of creativity and innovation.

Most recently, Richard Florida reported on this dynamic extensively in *Rise of the Creative Class*, as well as his follow-up work, *Flight of the Creative Class*. Florida's work meticulously documents the connection between hubs of creativity and regional prosperity. In those communities where creativity is highest, diversity is recognized not just as a closely held value but as a way of life. Decades earlier, in the 1969 book *The Economy of Cities*, Jane Jacobs put forward the hypothesis that not only does diversity provide a more favorable environment for economic development, it also fuels innovation— radical thinking for its time. In fact, the late Charles Abrams, considered to be one of the most influential "public intellectuals" of his era, stated in a *New York Times Book Review* piece on Jacobs's work, "The book is timely . . . and if it will irritate some of the experts it will also help bring some neglected issues and theories into public focus."[8]

In the study of the role international cities such as London, Paris, New York, and Tokyo play in the development and health of the global economy, their common feature of diversity is viewed as the actual engine of their economic growth.[9] As microcosms of this dynamic, G Quotient environments reflect on and draw strength from the individual talents and background of each stakeholder. Beyond the demographic makeup of their workforces, G Quotient environments also have leaders who act as advocates for broadening the diversity of clients, customers, and suppliers. In Jane Jacobs's last book, *Systems of Survival* (written in 1992), her message was as effective as it was simple: go around the city, observe how the world works, and look at reality in a new way.[10] My research found that G Quotient managers are doing just that in each of the four business sectors I studied. As a result, they are building workplace environments that reflect real-world diversity, because it's indeed a brand new neighborhood.

Inclusion Is Profitable

In 1911, Frederick Taylor opened the first chapter of *The Principles of Scientific Management* with the following statement: "The principal object of management should be to secure the maximum prosperity for the employer, coupled with the maximum prosperity for each employee." Often referred to as the original best-seller on business leadership, Taylor's book united this statement with the acknowledgment that most employers and employees engage in war rather than peace, and that perhaps the majority on either side do not believe that it's possible to arrange their "mutual relations" in order to bring their respective interests into complete alignment.

Obviously the call for inclusion in the workplace is nothing new. There have always been managers who rely on intimidation, discipline, and even the overt or implied threat of being fired to "engage" employees into action. Likewise, on the other end of the good boss–bad boss continuum, there have always been managers who motivate, respect, and value their employees as their preferred platform for engagement. However, what is new is the expectations of today's workforce. Changed as a result of employee reconstruction, contemporary workers no longer respond to leaders who cannot or will not acknowledge their individual value. Why? Because when you are empowered, the thought of not being valued is at war with your framework of sensibilities. The G Quotient works in alignment with this precept because managers with a high level of GQ recognize that in today's workplace, *people* rather than products are what drives companies to become successful and stay successful.

Jim Quigley understands the connection between employees feeling valued and the bottom line. As CEO of Deloitte & Touche USA LLP, one of the world's largest and most successful audit, tax, and consulting firms, Quigley is outspoken on the connection between his company's commitment to inclusion and the bottom line. His leadership mantra continually asserts that his employees must feel their ideas are valued—not irrespective of their individual identities but because of them.

This bold commitment has made a deep and positive impact on company profits. Initiatives within the company to create an environment of value, one where employees feel they can achieve because of their own individuality, have saved millions of dollars in recruiting and training costs. One program in particular, Deloitte Career Connections, which facilitates an inclusive approach to helping employees strengthen their careers within the company, has saved Deloitte more than $14 million.[11]

Inclusive workplace environments create greater organizational wealth. *Fortune* reports that the hundred best companies to work for in the United States have substantially higher stock market returns than the S&P 500 as a group.[12] Appreciating G Quotient leadership as a way to increase profits and shareholder value begins with understanding how to motivate employees without invoking hierarchal authority. For now, simply recognize that when G Quotient leaders flatten their immediate playing field, their employees gain the security and freedom to contribute beyond the status quo, which in turn heats up creativity, productivity, and profits.

Measuring the impact that inclusive environments have on the bottom line is admittedly a challenging task. To meet this challenge, Accenture recently developed a tool called the "Human Capital Development Framework." This unique measurement system is designed to determine, among other things, the actual financial benefit derived by offering employees an inclusive and affirming workplace environment.

For most organizations, it's relatively easy to measure quality, brand loyalty, even creativity. These areas can be readily quantified. For example, if an organization wants to assess its overall creativity, it doesn't have to look too far beyond the number of new products currently in development or recently launched. A 2005 white paper report on the successful results of the Accenture framework provides empirical evidence that organizations who put people first finish first. The report states that by focusing on three primary areas, defined as human capital strategy, employee development, and the workplace environment itself, organizations can position themselves to outperform their competition. On the basis of these beta test results, implemented in organizations representing a wide variety of fields and industries all around the world, it's already possible to say that effective human capital processes lead to better financial performance through enhanced leadership, workforce performance, employee engagement, and innovation.[13]

Further indication of this positive relationship is evidenced in a 2004 study conducted by James Oakley, a business professor at Purdue University. Oakley studied a hundred employees at American companies, investigating corporate culture. His research identified a positive link between employee satisfaction and customer satisfaction, and between customer satisfaction and profits. Oakley's findings suggest strong evidence that employees with a high level of job satisfaction can translate into satisfied customers—ultimately resulting in the improved financial performance of the organization. His research cites employee satisfaction as the primary source of employee engagement, suggesting that keeping the lines of communication open between management and employees is the most important factor in achieving satisfaction.[14]

Happiness Matters

A large majority of modern life is spent working on work. Allowing for two weeks of vacation and based on a minimum forty-hour work week (recent studies reported by the National Sleep Foundation estimate the average U.S. work week to be closer to forty-six hours, with 38 percent of employees working more than fifty hours) workers dedicate at least two thousand hours to their employers every year. Over a period of forty years this represents eighty thousand hours in the workplace. When you include the time spent sleeping, say seven hours a night over the same forty years, together that's a combined total of 181,000 hours or approximately *twenty-one years* doing nothing but work and sleep. I recently cited this statistic while speaking to a group of MBA students at a conference in Boston. Their reaction was unanimous—gaping mouths and shaking heads. One young man from MIT echoed what the rest of his colleagues seemed to be thinking silently to themselves, "Believe me," he said, "there's no way I'm giving a quarter of my life to an employer who doesn't think they need me just as much as I need them." Self-serving? Not at all. His employer *will* need him—as an engaged and happy employee. Otherwise, it's unlikely he will add any value to the organization—and instead will become a drain on its resources. Inclusiveness, engagement, and happiness represent the ultimate management trifecta in the recalibrated workplace.

The World Values Survey (WVS) is one of the most important ongoing research projects that has ever been undertaken and implemented. Measuring the values and beliefs in countries on all continents, it has measured the perspectives and experiences of nearly 80 percent of the world's total population. Four waves of research were carried out between 1981 and 2004, with the most recent going out into the field in 2005. The investigators are a diverse group of scientists from all around the globe, and their work on this project speaks to the magnitude of just how globalized and connected our society has become.

Ronald Inglehart, a professor of political science at the University of Michigan and one of the researchers who developed the WVS, addresses among hundreds of other issues the link between human happiness and prosperity. He found that in the United States and other countries where the majority of the population doesn't live under horrendous conditions of daily hunger and economic insecurity, there is a continual shift toward the need to belong, self-express, and have a participating role in society.[15]

In harmony with today's empowered employees, gay leaders believe that happiness matters. This represents a departure from last century's archetypal management philosophy where employees were purposely made to feel like replaceable cogs in the corporate wheel. The old adage, "A happy worker is a productive worker," takes on quite a different meaning in the recalibrated workplace.

In the Industrial Age, the translation of this particular sentiment included keeping employees in the dark as a means of organizational control. Leaders who subscribed to this management belief system wanted their employees to know very little about what was actually going on in the company and to a greater extent, in the field or industry. The desire to maintain complete control of organizational knowledge goes hand-in-hand with the Wizard of Oz syndrome, with organizational leaders seeking to portray themselves as bigger and better than they actually are. Because that choice has been taken off the table by instant access to specialized work-related knowledge, the workplace happiness of today's employees is directly connected to their own sense of belonging to and participating in an environment where they perceive themselves as key to the organization itself.

In teaching my business communication course, I spend a great deal of time on human behavior theories because, after all, organizations are made up of human beings. One of the communication models that clearly and simply demonstrates the valuable dynamics associated with being "in the know" is represented in a model called the Johari Window. A mainstay communication behavior model since it was developed in the 1950s, it has over the last few years experienced a national resurgence in popularity due to the importance now being placed on what were once considered soft skills in the workplace.

In very simplistic terms, the Johari Window is divided into four panes, each representing various levels of personal awareness. For example, I may be aware of something that is unknown to you and vice versa. The lesson it illustrates is that successful relationships occur only if there is a balance between self-disclosure and feedback. For effective communication to occur, including that within the manager-employee relationship, it's imperative to open the hidden portion of the window, where information that is unknown to one or even both parties becomes open and known to both parties. As a basic tenet of interpersonal communication, if you're not an insider, you're an outsider, and employees need to know they are in that window pane of shared information if they are to become full organizational participants. Basically, it's about belonging. As a state of being in the workplace, I found, belonging is fundamentally tied to happiness, which is very much a by-product of shared interpersonal communication. As such, it can only be realized when the organizational window is fully open.

Advancing a New Type of Power

One of the great Peter Drucker's most famous quotes compares employees to an orchestra, suggesting that they are to be conducted and not bossed. In G Quotient environments, employees have the freedom and security to go to their boss for direction and guidance, recognized as a hallmark of effective leadership since Frederick Taylor wrote his 1911 best-seller. And for anyone who may be thinking at this point in the book that G Quotient leadership places employees in charge of the organization, I'd like you to consider that it's the person others go to for direction and guidance who actually holds the most power. In the context of the recalibrated workplace, successful leadership is about being powerful in a different way, one that stems from respect and value for others rather than hierarchy and job titles.

The Tata Group, one of the rising stars in the global economy, has built an empire by understanding this new type of power. It's a relatively new conglomerate that's proving that marketplace prosperity and placing utmost value on employees are intrinsically tied together in a recipe for international success. With eighty different businesses to date and revenues in excess of $17 billion, it has tripled its earnings over the last decade. Just since the beginning of the new century, Tata Group's parent company, Tata Sons, has purchased well-known companies that include Tetley Tea, Daewoo Motors, and NatSteel, gaining additional footing in Britain, South Korea, and Singapore respectively. This India-based company was built on principles rooted in its country's struggle for independence from Britain and the influence of early-twentieth-century Fabian socialists, and it is widely known to be beyond the reach of India's own corrupt political environment. In fact, it's considered to be a waste of time to even think about bribing any of the company's top leadership for corporate favortism.[16]

Ratan Tata, the Cornell University–educated CEO of the Tata Group, approaches leadership with a fierce sense of responsibility toward his employees. For example, when cutting the workforce of

Tata Steel, he was steadfast in his decision to keep laid-off workers on full salary until retirement. Of course that kind of employee loyalty would be cost-prohibitive in other nations, but in India it is feasible—though rare. As the company's chief leader, Tata believes it speaks to the core of his success, refusing to succeed, as he says, "over everybody's dead bodies."[17] He is an active manager in nearly all his company's businesses, and his own belief system is what drives his direct involvement. The Tata Group places two-thirds of its equity into philanthropic trusts—the only company of its size and stature to do so—and it distributes between 8 percent and 14 percent of its net profits every year to charities. In 2005, Tata stated that he believes his sense of obligation to other people serves to enhance his leadership abilities as well as increasing shareholder value, contributing to what he believes is "a greater quality of life that benefits all."[18]

On the domestic front, in 2001, when Dan Carp, then chairman and CEO of Eastman Kodak Company, announced his transformation strategy to turn the company around after limping into the Digital Age, he made it clear that workplace inclusion had to play a key role in repositioning the fading corporate giant. As one of Carp's core strategies for beginning the process of reinvention, he maintained that the company's future relied on emphasizing dignity and respect for all of Kodak's constituencies.[19]

Initial skepticism on Wall Street about Kodak's ability to redefine itself as a digital company has been replaced with tempered optimism about the company's future. Despite an increase in corporate revenues to $13.5 billion in 2004, the company still faced what can only be described as an uphill struggle to remain profitable as it continued to revamp itself into a digital company. Even so, in 2005 Kodak dominated the U.S. digital camera market (with 23.8 percent market share) over both Canon and Sony. For the June 2005 quarter, earnings from continuing operations were $160 million on revenues of $3.69 billion, representing a 6 percent increase. Digital sales rose an impressive 43 percent in the same quarter, edging Wall Street's tempered enthusiasm a little closer to bullish.[20]

Regardless of the final outcome, one of the most interesting elements of Kodak as a business case is the front-row seat inclusiveness it has maintained in its comeback strategy. Never before has a company the size of Kodak placed such visibly high importance on inclusiveness as an ingredient for success. Now under the leadership of Antonio Perez, the company continues to pursue its former crown with *inclusiveness* remaining a chief priority in its overall plan of action.

Mistakes Can Lead to Innovation

At the beginning of each semester, I hold a roundtable discussion in the classroom about the various leadership styles that play out in organizations. When the subject of motivation comes up, the conversation inevitably turns to Douglas McGregor, the renowned social psychologist who developed the famous X-Y management theory nearly a half-century ago, describing two types of managers. The X-type manager believes that employees are innately lazy, and that unless forced with the threat of punishment they will not be productive at work. These managers are typically more than eager to find someone to blame for failures or problems. Y-type managers on the other hand, believe that employees are innately self-directed and will work toward their professional objectives without the threat of punishment.[21]

In keeping with McGregor's theory, X-type managers typically provide feedback to employees based on what's been done wrong instead of right. This dynamic isn't necessarily tied to the personality flaws of all X-type managers; it's simply the continuation of negative training messages that we begin receiving in childhood. For example, as children we're scolded for making mistakes—by parents, teachers, and peers. Even though much of our learning at early ages is the result of making what might be colossal blunders, we nonetheless become socialized to *avoid* making mistakes. In grammar school, for example, raising one's hand and then giving the wrong answer may bring smirks and sighs from other students.

The message we receive in those settings is clearly that making mistakes results in public ridicule. But we're not talking about hurt feelings in the context of business leadership. We're talking about profits—and not catching and correcting mistakes as soon as possible can cost big money.

Creating a workplace environment where mistakes aren't viewed as the equivalent of failure also promotes greater opportunities to improve and therefore advance the organization. The result of casting mistakes in any other context can halt organizational growth as well as block employers from the necessary loop of communication between themselves and employees that plays a vital role in successful leadership.

In *Will Your Next Mistake Be Fatal?* Wharton School of Business professor Robert E. Mittelstaedt Jr. documents how sequences of mistakes lead to corporate and even political disasters. He states that if the chain of mistakes is not broken early on, the damage and cost will rise exponentially. From the Watergate break-in to Coca-Cola's disastrous New Coke campaign in the 1980s to the Enron debacle, not admitting and correcting mistakes has threatened not just a fall from grace but near or complete destruction.[22] Mittelstaedt believes that organizational culture, greatly defined by where leaders fall on the X-Y management scale, is not only a powerful organizational influence but ultimately dangerous, as in the case of Enron. Mittelstaedt's research cites Enron's leaders' belief that they were "more intelligent, insightful and skilled" than everyone else— including their employees, and suggests that mistakes made by the company were the direct result of the "culture of supremacy" built by its leaders.

I go down this road for a reason—environments based on arrogance, just like those based on inclusion, are defined by more than one leadership principle or behavior. Each organization is a system of many types of behaviors, each typically a reflection of the greater environment cultivated by organizational leaders. In other words, the likelihood of the leadership of Enron as described by Mittelstaedt embracing G Quotient principles would be slim.

When employees are afraid to talk to the boss out of fear of being punished for making a mistake, they naturally tend to hide problems until they may no longer be fixable. This type of workplace fear inhibits risk taking, stifling both creativity and its best byproduct, innovation. Leo Burnett, the famous marketing expert who built an advertising dynasty on the invention of evocative campaigns that made household names out of corporate identities ranging from the Jolly Green Giant to the Pillsbury Doughboy, once said, "To swear off making mistakes is very easy. All you have to do is swear off having ideas." When managers motivate instead of dictate, mistakes surface sooner rather than later. As a result, they are *fixed* sooner, saving the organization money and minimizing the risk for public embarrassment.

Employees Need to Own Their Jobs

G Quotient leaders view job ownership as something that should ideally be held by employees themselves. Based on individual levels of expertise, this particular type of ownership grants employees primary authority over their specific areas of responsibility within the organization. This isn't to say that an employee who repeatedly makes poor decisions will continue to be afforded the same level of job ownership. Rather, it's about the belief that when empowered employees are entrusted with this type of opportunity for workplace authority, they become more involved in their work and more committed to professional excellence. Why? Because we all want more autonomy over our own lives—including our jobs.

Jim Collins, the renowned management researcher and author, found that good-to-great companies created a consistent system of management, and then gave employees the autonomy and responsibility to perform their own jobs within this system.[23] It's also been proven that the benefits associated with this type of job ownership can extend beyond the workplace and into an employee's life away from the organization. In 2005, the American Psychological Association found that employees who are entrusted with autonomy in the workplace were also more likely to bring home positive psychological benefits as a result.[24]

As a researcher, I see that much of the information I acquire about the benefits associated with employees owning and therefore being responsible for their own jobs is often reflected in the reasons people also cite for leaving jobs. In fact, some of the most valuable feedback I've received is from employees in G Quotient environments who compare their current positive experience to previous ones in less ideal settings. The overarching lesson to be learned from all this recounting of experiences is that most managers don't even begin to recognize the impact they have on the lives of their employees. Consider, for example, the following excerpt from an off-the-record interview I conducted with a very accomplished woman from a Fortune 100 company. Now employed in a G Quotient environment, she describes her previous manager as "abusive." Ironically, it's within the same organization.

> After just a few months reporting to this particular executive, I realized that I would never be allowed to act on any of my own ideas. By the end of the first year, I had resigned myself to having no professional voice. As a manager with several employees, it made life even more difficult because I had no authority to give my staff any direction. Whenever I'd meet with my previous manager, sometimes I just wanted to come right out and say, "Tell me what you want me to do and how you want me to do it, because we both know I don't have the slightest say in the direction of my own area of responsibility." But instead, we always went through this ridiculous meeting process that always ended up with me simply becoming a robot.

As an educated professional, she told me, she knew she had to get out because she was beginning to forget how to do great work. Overall, her time in this particular setting lasted eighteen months, and half of that was spent trying to transfer into another department. "To be honest," she said, "when I was in that situation, doing a good job had no meaning to me. Instead, I felt creatively and emotionally abused."

While most companies were very accommodating in allowing their employees to be interviewed on the record, because this particular interview describes a less-than-motivational manager who is still employed in the same organization, I was not given permission to use the name of the employee or the company. What I can disclose is that, also speaking off the record, one official said, "[This particular manager] is like a headless nail. It's been impossible to pry him out." And if you feel that *abused* is too strong a word for this particular situation, it's nonetheless an accurate description of how passionately empowered employees feel about being granted ownership over their professional roles. It's that personal.

9

TEN THINGS EVERY MANAGER NEEDS TO KNOW ABOUT G QUOTIENT LEADERSHIP

Flying from Los Angeles to Portland recently to speak at a career expo, I was very pleased when it looked like there wouldn't be anyone seated next to me. For anyone who travels on a regular basis, I'm sure you'll agree, a vacancy in the adjacent seat is almost as good as an upgrade. You can put up the armrest, spread out and actually have enough space to be comfortable. Then, with just a few minutes to spare before takeoff, a hurried-looking gentleman armed with a briefcase and laptop rushed onto the plane and of course, into the empty seat. Based on appearances, he was right out of central casting for what can best be described as a stereotypical middle-aged conservative businessman. Classic Brooks Brothers suit, starched white shirt with monogrammed cuffs, and a slightly expanded waistline from too many late-night business dinners. I'll admit I thought I had him all figured out. We exchanged a few initial pleasantries and then became engaged in our own work.

Soon after the flight attendant served lunch, my seatmate noticed a promotional flyer amid my paperwork for the career expo I was headed to in Portland. Sponsored by Portland State University, it was an event that brought together lesbian, gay, bisexual, and transgender college students from PSU as well as other colleges and universities in the Pacific Northwest. "Do you know the names of the companies that will be there?" he asked? Since this was really our first exchange beyond making comments about the weather, it took me a moment to realize I'd been asked a legitimate question.

Always ready to talk about anything related to my work, I told him it was less of a recruiting event and more focused on empowering students to recognize their own professional value. He asked how I was involved, and I told him that I was giving the keynote speech the following morning. Remember when I thought I had him all figured out? I was about to learn a much-needed lesson on books and their covers.

As it turns out, he was an executive at a well-known investment banking firm in New York who was on his way to solve a diversity-related personnel problem at the company's Portland office. He also told me that he had been in Los Angeles visiting his daughter who recently graduated from UCLA. In fact, his daughter was the reason why he was curious about companies that might be attending the career expo. Without any hesitation, he shared with me that his daughter was gay and that he was concerned about her getting into a good company. Yes, a very big lesson indeed.

For the remainder of the flight, we chatted about our mutual workplace interests, and I made some suggestions about potential employers that I thought might help his daughter. Offering his perspective on Wall Street's views about diversity and inclusiveness, he said, "I have a very difficult time convincing my firm's (mostly) white male leadership that expanding the 'types' of people around the executive table won't force them out of their own jobs." He told me that even though he continues to stress that diversity and inclusiveness simply meant that the firm would need to get what he called a "larger table," most of his colleagues refused to hear his message. In the meantime, he said, "I go around the country putting out fires because they refuse to change." He went on to say that he believes this type of reluctance is ultimately based on lack of understanding and insight, adding, "For most of the people in charge on Wall Street, diversity represents the potential to lose control over their professional domain. It's unfamiliar waters."

In developing this particular chapter, therefore, my goal was to capture and convey ten important "need-to-know" qualities of G Quotient leadership in order to increase understanding and insight. To do so, I found it necessary to address the G Quotient both conceptually as a leadership paradigm and also in the tangible actions of G Quotient leaders themselves. Based on surveys, interviews, and field research, each of these ten "need-to-know" points represents an opportunity to gain a greater sense of familiarity about the attributes and benefits of G Quotient leadership.

1. *G Quotient leadership is both objective and subjective.*

Male and female. Gay and straight. Objective and subjective. Eastern religions teach the value of balance as being a source of happiness and long-lasting success, personally as well as professionally. At first glance, you may have decoded these combinations as polar opposites rather than as complementary pairs. Of course, neither is good and neither is bad—just examples of opposing forces that we use to define the world we live in as well as our approach to life.

Yin-yang philosophy teaches that even though opposing forces exist, they cycle together to create harmony, and we should be cautious in viewing either force as more desirable than the other. As a leadership paradigm, the G Quotient does not separate the various processes of management as completely objective or subjective. Rather, I found, gay executives are objective in their examination of relevant workplace data and subjective in their judgment of that data based on the seven G Quotient principles.

Alan Watts dedicated his life to the study of Eastern thought and religion. In *Tao: The Watercourse Way*, still one of the world's most important books on interpreting Eastern philosophy for Western cultures more than thirty years after its first publication, Watts describes this concept with brilliant simplicity: "My inside arises mutually with my outside and though the two may differ they cannot be separated."[1] Similarly, gay executives appear to have balanced both internal and external forces to create a fully integrated (and balanced) management belief system.

Rather than trying to balance people, processes, and final outcomes, gay executives move their organizations forward by balancing *employee needs*, *organizational needs*, and *customer needs*. Once these collective needs are identified and acknowledged, the processes of the organization (as described in the next need-to-know) can be developed based on this recognition. In G Quotient environments, developing organizational processes that incorporate the needs of these three major interest groups provides highly effective guidelines for doing business. These organizations and working units face fewer potential land mines because this particular type of balance is highly conducive to staying in touch with the demands of the marketplace. When organizational processes and outcomes are viewed as functions of the needs of these three interest groups, as those needs shift and change, so can organizational goals. At the end of the day, this particular type of balance provides managers with a greater opportunity to deliver products and services that are consistently more relevant and timely than the competition's offerings.

2.   G *Quotient leadership focuses on the processes of work rather than the final product.*

While waiting in line recently for coffee and pastry at my favorite morning hangout, certainly not the healthiest breakfast but nonetheless satisfying, I found myself immersed in the process of how this bakery's mega-calorie cinnamon rolls are manufactured. As a very effective marketing strategy, the owner has constructed the order line to back up along a large display window into the room where employees create and then deliver their temptations into baker's bins—all before the customers' eyes.

At the time, since I was engulfed in assembling and tabulating research, many of my regular routines seemed to take on new meaning. Essentially, everything became a case study. The dry cleaner was all about command-and-control management. The supermarket served as a model for team building. And on this particular morning, my favorite bakery became a living illustration of the dynamics of the process versus the final product. Being in this particular frame of mind, I noticed that above all else, the bakery's employees appeared to be having a great time. Preparing a new batch of their locally famous cinnamon rolls, they laughed and bantered while rolling out the dough mixture, cutting and shaping each batch until it was just right. Finally, with a bit of dramatic flair, they coated their creations with sugar and then placed them in a shiny stainless-steel oven.

From an organizational perspective, what became clear to me is that most of the energy and enthusiasm in this particular environment was derived from the *process of work* rather than the product itself. In fact, when the product was actually removed from the oven, it was with relatively little fanfare. However, as soon as the employees returned to their central process, which in this case was making cinnamon rolls, their vigor and energy immediately returned.

Industrial Age paradigms taught managers to focus almost exclusively on the final product, to the extent that employees weren't encouraged or even allowed to enjoy the processes of their work. In the bakery scenario I just described, it's quite the opposite. Aligned with the needs of empowered employees, workers in process-focused G Quotient environments interpret that focus in the following way: "Since the process of work is all about people, and leadership focuses more on the process than the final product, then I must be of primary value." Not surprising, I found that it isn't actually the end result that gives the most satisfaction to employees in G Quotient environments, but rather the process of creating or doing.

In practice, when managers get too wrapped up in the final product, their focus shifts from their employees to the product. Notice the connection with the first need-to-know item in this list. The balance of forces is a consistent G Quotient theme that I didn't fully appreciate until I put all my research connections together.

So, with the responsibility of creating and sustaining successful and engaged processes of work securely resting in the manager's corner, the responsibility for the final product rests with *both* the manager and employees. Frankly, it doesn't matter if the final product is a cinnamon roll or a luxury car, this dynamic remains the same. What's important to recognize is that while responsibility for the final product is *shared* with employees, I found the gay executives identified in my research retained primary *accountability*. In other words, it's the manager's reputation and presumably job on the line if the final product is anything less than superior. Whatever happens on their watch, these executives typically believed that success as well as failure is directly tied to their own leadership performance, because they were the ones in charge of the organization.

3. *G Quotient leadership models a systems approach to management.*

A system consists of multiple interactive parts that together form one greater whole. Certainly there is nothing more complex than a human being. In the workplace, where many human beings connect as one greater whole under the umbrella of the employing organization, the overarching goal of this particular system is to work in harmony to achieve a common mission.

In general, all systems are built up from the complexity and interdependence of relationships. Ludwig von Bertalanffy is generally considered to be the founder of what's known in academic circles as the *systems theory,* which in spite of its scholarly name is simply about adopting a functional approach to problem solving that can be used effectively in all types of disciplines—including business leadership. A biologist by profession, von Bertalanffy developed his systems approach to problem solving for use in scientific fields, and it first gained acceptance where quantitative analysis was most prevalent. In fact, from 1955 to 1958, von Bertalanffy was even a visiting professor at USC, where he reached beyond his professional comfort zone to be one of the first to apply a systems approach to addressing issues in both psychology and the social sciences. Interestingly, in my own field, after nearly a hundred years of various theories being put forth to explain why and how people make career decisions at different stages throughout their lives, many professionals (including me) have adopted a systems approach in the last decade simply as a response to the complexity of the contemporary workplace.

Leadership can be either a closed system, where interaction with the workplace environment makes no impact on the processes of work, or an open system, where interaction makes a significant impact. G Quotient leadership is unquestionably an open system, because these leaders are constantly influenced by interaction with the workplace environment itself. In this context, they are constantly assessing how employees, the greater organization, and—last but not least—customers and clients also interact with the environment.

4. *G Quotient leadership places value on experiential learning.*

As a leadership paradigm, the G Quotient includes the belief that what employees do in the workplace is more vital to the success of the greater organization than what they know. David A. Kolb, the renowned Harvard-educated social theorist, is a pioneer on the subject of experiential learning. As one of the foremost experts in the field, he describes experiential learning as a four-phase cycle in which the learner begins by doing something concrete or having a specific experience, which provides a basis for the learner's observation and reflection on the experience and formation of a response to it. These observations are then assimilated into a conceptual framework or related to other concepts in the learner's past experience and knowledge. From that basis, implications for action can be derived and then tested and applied in different situations.[2] What does that really mean? *People learn by doing.*

Empowered employees are well matched for the precepts of experiential learning. Because so much knowledge already exists in our brains as a result of life in the Digital Age, without practical application it just sits idle. And when knowledge isn't used, it becomes a source of frustration. In the new world of work, if employees aren't able to benefit and ultimately move forward based on their own knowledge, then the four-phase cycle described by Kolb is disrupted. Gay executives recognize that without practical application and the feedback generated from an open system of communication, there's simply no way to hone skills or, more to the point, develop new ones.

While analyzing the literally hundreds of surveys and spreadsheets scattered all over the floor of my office one day, I realized that one of the reasons gay executives are generating such high levels of employee engagement is connected to the same dynamic often experienced by college students participating in internships.

These executives turn on the lights for their people so they will grow professionally.

The practical definition of experiential learning is simple: transforming knowledge into skill through the act of doing. In my research, I found that gay executives widely believe the best way for employees to become experts at what they do is through an ongoing, one-two combination of workplace experience and evaluation. As an interesting note of conclusion on this subject, in G Quotient settings, the evaluation process also played a significant role in employee engagement. In addition to providing employees with feedback about their job performance, gay executives solicited first-person reviews from employees themselves. By bringing employees in on their own evaluation process, this practice appeared to generate greater buy-in when setting new goals for the future, further connecting employees to the organization as well as their own professional development.

5. *G Quotient leadership focuses on the present.*

One of the ironic twists in my findings is that while the past played an enormous role in the evolution of gay executives, putting them in the right place at the right time, these leaders spend little time looking over one shoulder at the road behind them. Instead, what I found was a common commitment to focus on the present as a means to prepare for the future. In metaphorical terms, the present may be our bridge between the past and the future, but in today's constant context of change, the past can easily become dead weight that keeps us from moving forward. For most gay executives, success is achieved by viewing past accomplishments as points of reference rather than as models for continued achievement. They turn to foresight, surveying the ground ahead to avoid any pitfalls—something gay men in particular have learned as a survival skill, as discussed in this book's Introduction.

How do you know if you spend too much time in the past? A professor in my graduate communications program once told me that it's possible to determine how much time people spend communicating with the past based on how they react to a near-miss traffic accident. One day in class, he said, "Let's suppose you're headed down the freeway at a fairly high speed of travel, and suddenly you look up and see an ocean of brake lights and swerving cars. In the blur of a microsecond, you begin to hear metal slamming into metal, but somehow manage to maneuver your car out of the tangled mess. It's over as quickly as it began, and you are completely untouched, still heading toward your original destination. However, in the rearview mirror you see several cars piled up in the middle of the freeway and realize that you were nearly in the middle of what might have been a fatal traffic accident."

I vividly remember this particular professor, a very imposing man in his late sixties with a full head of snow-white hair. This particular example has stuck with me for so long because when he presented it in class, he suddenly turned to me and asked, "How do you react, Snyder? Do you spend the rest of the day, perhaps even weeks and months, thinking about what would have happened if you weren't able to escape the accident? Or do you consider yourself extremely fortunate, perhaps even saying a prayer of thanks to a higher power, and then go on with the events of your day?"

At the time, aside from being annoyed that I had been singled out in class, I remember thinking to myself how generalized this hypothesis seemed and that it had little relevance to the subject of communication. However, I'm sure I picked the latter reaction, since it's more my nature to shrug things off and keep going. I hadn't thought about this hypothesis for years until it came to life in a very real way.

As part of a task force hired to advise a large engineering company about a flurry of harassment and discrimination suits brought against them by numerous employees, I was invited to sit in on several meetings and staff interviews designed to identify why the environment in one particular department had become increasingly hostile and intolerant. In addition to me and two other consultants, the task force included an attorney from an outside law firm hired to provide specialized feedback to the company about potential liability. The law firm engaged for this assignment turned out to be located near my home, and since the engineering company's head-quarters was well over an hour away, the attorney and I decided to share a ride to one of our meetings.

I was more than pleased when she offered to drive. As we were about to get on the freeway, however, we experienced one of those near misses my professor had referred to in his classroom. It isn't likely this particular accident would have been fatal, but it most certainly could have been nasty. For the rest of the day, including our trip back home, I repeatedly heard, "What if we had been in that accident? We might be in the hospital right now." Over and over, she said, "My new car would have been completely destroyed." You can imagine my surprise when she even told me that her assistant would probably "enjoy" hearing news that she was laid up in the hospital. At the end of the day, just glad to be home and out of her car, I tried to put this unfortunate experience out of my mind.

Several weeks later, I received an unexpected voice mail from this same woman asking me to lunch. In her message she said that she was leaving her law firm and needed some professional advice about her next career move. At first I hesitated based on the less-than-enjoyable time I had during our previous encounter, but something in her voice compelled me to accept her invitation. Frankly, I was more than curious about why she decided to leave a firm that had quickly gained a stand-out reputation for integrity and innovation. At any rate, as our conversation unfolded over lunch, she told me she couldn't endure working for a firm that conducted business in "new and unorthodox" ways. In her worldview, "new and unortho-dox" was primarily about how the firm employed the Internet and other digital technologies to market itself as a twenty-first-century law firm.

Rather than examining how she could adapt to these changes, she was adamant about getting away from them. For someone barely in her fifties, she was surprisingly desperate to hang on to what she termed the "tried-and-true ways of the profession." The embodiment of my communication professor's hypothesis, this woman was so consumed by holding on to the past that it was nearly impossible for her to focus on the present, much less prepare for the future. As a result, her career was in serious trouble.

Whether an innate personality characteristic or something that's learned, in the context of business leadership, recognizing that past success isn't always relevant to future success is critical to being an effective leader. Based on the career health of the gay executives identified in my research, being able to let the past go and move on appears to open the door to creativity and innovation as well as to a variety of other types of professional possibilities that might otherwise get trapped in the "what might have been" mentality.

6.   G *Quotient leaders are still in the trenches.*

The message that's heard when leaders stand side by side with their employees is one of *equality*. For employees, this message is that they are a meaningful part of the organization. For managers, it's ultimately about the importance of remaining part of the team and not turning into a disembodied voice calling out from the executive suite, ordering employees to perform. It's motivational leadership in action.

Politics is full of stories about elected officials thrown out of office as a result of being out of touch with the problems of real people. In fact, today's empowered employees morally object to leadership that smacks of elitism. In this context, it isn't so much about getting your own coffee as it is about respecting the work of others. Being in the trenches means that you care enough about your employees and your organization to pay attention to their work and lend a hand when appropriate. At the end of the day it's about respect.

When managers are removed from the mechanics of their employees' work and allow themselves to be perceived as having little or no knowledge about the processes of the work, it's difficult for employees to be motivated when they receive direction. Typically, in these types of environments, the "do as I say, not as I do" philosophy is equal to a death sentence for employee morale because direction is interpreted as orders.

As a point in contrast, a colleague recently told me a story from the trenches about her boss, who happens to be a good friend of mine. I had never heard this story and of course, it's always amusing to hear tales about a friend's workplace behavior. Throughout my career, I have had the good fortune to be inspired by a handful of quality professionals who have taught me a great deal about effective leadership. The friend I'm speaking of is Katharine Harrington, dean of admissions and financial aid at USC, who is unquestionably one of these quality professionals. A former professor of business ethics, Katharine once found that her leadership role at the university required her to iron wrinkled USC tablecloths on the floor of a hotel conference room.

Here's what happened: she was on a recruiting trip to speak with potential students and their parents in Arizona, and she walked into the hotel conference room to find that the staff had unpacked what must have been the world's most rumpled tablecloths and simply placed them on the tables that were set up all around the room. But chatting across tables covered in what looked like something pulled from a clothes hamper was far from acceptable for a group that would be seen as the face of the university. So with only a slight window of time before the beginning of the event, Katharine and her staff immediately went to their rooms and armed themselves with well-worn hotel irons. Using the floor as a makeshift ironing board, they pressed each tablecloth right up to the beginning of what turned out to be a very successful event. The person who recounted this story also told me that her own morale went through the roof after that experience because her boss was down there on the floor ironing like everybody else. Why? Because it added to the value of her own job. It's a real-world example of how equality-based connections can be developed between managers and employees.

7.   G Quotient leaders manage inspiration.

In 2003, the U.S. Library of Congress reported registering more than 530,000 copyrights for art, music, books, screenplays, and software. In that same year, the U.S. patent office received more than 365,000 applications for new products.[3] Without the freedom to focus on inspiration, imagine how many of humankind's greatest innovators—from Madame Curie to the Wright Brothers and beyond—would have been able to fulfill their own imaginings of what's possible. Certainly not every employee is going to change the world with something as monumental as X-ray machines or airplanes, but relative to their own field and ambitions, their collective contributions could easily transform most any economy into a superpower.

Since 2002, the Chicago Innovation Awards has annually honored those companies making meaningful improvements in our lives, based on the level of innovation or uniqueness they offer.[4] Sponsored by the Wrigley Company, each year the program honors ten companies. According to a 2005 article in the *Chicago Sun-Times*, if you collectively take the thirty companies honored from 2002 through 2004 and create a mutual fund made up of the same companies, you can actually measure the value of innovation. If you assume an initial investment of $1,000 in each of the publicly traded honorees (with stock purchased one month prior to receiving their award), this particular mutual fund would have returned a 30 percent rate of return—outperforming the Dow Jones Industrial Average's paltry 7 percent over the same period of time.[5]

Sometimes the result of brainstorming, sometimes of desperation or even unknown origins, inspiration (professional or otherwise) can only come from a mind free to explore new types of thought. Louisa May Alcott, author of one of the most celebrated books in literary history, *Little Women*, once proclaimed, "Far away in the sunshine are my highest inspirations. I may not reach them, but I can look up and see the beauty, believe in them and try to follow where they lead." Because inspiration is often fleeting, it must be allowed to exist before it can be capitalized on.

Inspiration is typically defined as being somebody or something that ignites the human mind to creative thought. Gay executives see inspiration as a manageable commodity, and one critical to the success of an organization. What I found is that gay executives typically manage this particular commodity by creating environments where employees are not distracted by negativity, which can (and does) come in several forms—one of the most dangerous being negative energy directed toward the leader as an individual. Instead, by virtue of the seven G Quotient principles, I found that gay executives create environments where this type of negativity is relatively nonexistent. In *Now Discover Your Strengths* (2001), Marcus Buckingham and Donald Clifton emphasize that great organizations watch for clues about the talent of their employees in an effort to transform them into actual career strengths. When managers constantly focus on what's wrong with their employees rather than what's right, they lose the opportunity to develop employee talents that would ultimately result in not just inspiration but creativity and its by-product innovation as well.

When I'm submerged in the writing process, my own sources of inspiration are subject to change many times throughout the day. Some remain constant, such as the belief that this work matters, while others pop up without warning. For example, one day a phone call from a good friend who's employed in a hostile work environment reminded me how quickly negative leadership can completely shut down all potential to, as Alcott said, "look up and see the beauty."

My friend's voice at the other end of the phone was a combination of frustration, fury, and desperation. Her boss had just told her that she would be assuming the work of two people who recently resigned without any increase in salary. When my friend asked her boss about overload pay, her boss' response was basically to laugh in her face. After a bit of consoling, and then encouraging her to get out of this negative environment, I was struck by the pervasive loss generated by leadership committed to ruling rather than inspiring. Because my friend is someone who is typically inspired to achieve through her own creative ideas and endless enthusiasm, the loss of actual innovation as a result of her manager's behavior is truly immeasurable. From a much greater perspective, no one will ever know what has been sacrificed in terms of economic or even societal advancement because organizations and employees were not *inspired* to fully engage in their professional roles.

8.   G *Quotient leaders focus on positive employee characteristics.*

Positive psychology is a science devoted to the study of understanding and building on strengths and assets so as to facilitate happiness and success: focusing on what's right rather than what's wrong. The *American Psychologist* devoted its first issue of the twenty-first century to this emerging science.[6] Today, positive psychology has contributed to our appreciation of how positive emotions and character traits have served to advance both the individuals and organizations that embrace them.[7]

One of this science's founders and pioneers, Martin Seligman, professor of psychology at the University of Pennsylvania and former president of the American Psychological Association, identified six virtues representing twenty-four individual strengths that assist in the definition, cultivation, and measurement of positive character traits. Among the individual strengths are creativity, open-mindedness, authenticity, and fairness. Either explicitly or implicitly, these strengths are significantly represented in G Quotient leadership as practiced by gay executives. Without a conscious effort to subscribe to the science of positive psychology or, more to the point, even a probable awareness of its parameters, gay executives are demonstrating leadership behaviors that predominantly focus on what's *positive* about their employees, encouraging them to do the same with respect to their own colleagues and peers.

As a case in point, I recently had a conversation with the husband of a good friend who is entirely focused on what's wrong with his employees. Whenever a difficult situation or problem arises in his company, he blames the people who work for him. One night at dinner, I suggested that he try and identify what's right with his employees and that he could enhance his own success by better understanding the needs and expectations of his workforce. He had a very difficult time hearing my message because he's stuck in what I call the *employee blame cycle.* From his perspective, organizational problems are never related to the manager's own deficiency, because it's always the fault of employees.

Ongoing criticism of employees or a propensity to always focus on their inadequacies will in most cases outweigh any positives associated with the environment. Beyond the emotional quality of the workplace and loss of talent development, there's a great potential for loss of productivity associated with employees who seek to even the score. For example, "My boss never says anything positive to me so I'll take some extra time at lunch." Or, "I think I'll call in sick today because I just can't face all the negativity." In some extreme cases, basically honest people have even turned to stealing from their employers simply because they felt it was owed to them due to constant unfair criticism.

If you haven't felt this way yourself at some time in your professional life, illegal behavior aside, I'm sure you know others who have—and for the most part, justifiably so. Pervasive negativity is one of the most expensive drains that companies can experience and also one that is nearly impossible to measure. On the other hand, when there is an emphasis placed on the positive aspects of employees, people are likely to go the extra mile for their manager as well as the organization itself. It's a basic tenet of the human condition: the better we're treated, the better we treat others in return.

9.   G *Quotient leaders run their organizations like entrepreneurs.*

Small businesses have a rich history of changing the face of the world, in part because creativity and innovation are requirements for success in any new enterprise. On the flip side, getting new ideas through the approval process in most big businesses can drag on until they become old ideas. In any slow-to-react setting, the process of green-lighting new projects can take gut instinct completely out of the business equation—gut instinct being a fundamental ingredient of entrepreneurship.

Gay executives run their organizations very much like small businesses. These environments tend to promote a demonstrated commitment to implementing new ideas faster and more effectively than the competition, because entrepreneurs recognize the importance of exploiting gut instinct (or intuition) as a key to success.

The value of running an organization based on entrepreneurial ideals is reflected in the impressive statistics detailing the overwhelming productivity of small businesses. According to the Small Business Administration, small businesses produce 55 percent of all innovations in the United States, where the time line between gut instinct and final product is nearer weeks and months than years and decades. In 2005, 50 percent of the private workforce in the United States was employed by the country's 25 million small businesses. When you consider how this represents more than 50 percent of the U.S. gross national product, it's evident that the economy itself depends on the continuation of these entrepreneurial ideals.[8]

In general, I found that in G Quotient environments, creating an organizational culture based on the general philosophy and spirit of entrepreneurship also eliminated the need for gay executives to carry the entire weight of the working unit on their own shoulders. Particularly relative to the subject of granting job ownership to their employees, as explored in the second "need-to-know" in this chapter, gay executives in turn gain the professional freedom to focus on developing new business opportunities that ultimately benefit their employees, their organizations, and themselves.

10.   *G Quotient leaders understand and value themselves.*

In February 1891, Oscar Wilde wrote what turned out to be a very timely article for the *Fortnightly Review*, an influential publishing fixture of late Victorian society that attracted many of the most influential writers of the day. Ahead of its time in many respects, the *Fortnightly* began as a means to provide an open forum for discussing issues relevant to the era. This particular article of Wilde's was titled "The Soul of Man Under Socialism," and includes the following passage: "*Know thyself* was written over the portal of the antique world. Over the portal of the new world, *be thyself* shall be written."

The same year Wilde wrote these words, he became intimately involved with Lord Alfred Douglas, son of the Marquess of Queensberry. Ultimately, this relationship led to what became known as the "Queensberry Scandal," and Wilde was imprisoned in 1895 for what was termed an "act of indecency." When Wilde was released from prison in 1897, he was in poor health, and as a result of this very public scandal was forced to spend the remainder of his life in exile. When he died three years later at the age of forty-six, Wilde was penniless.

One of the common threads already discussed among the gay executives in my research is that they have all placed themselves in environments where they can succeed as themselves. In G Quotient settings, one of the paths to employee engagement and motivation can be connected to the authentic environments created by these leaders. The opposite of what Wilde experienced in his own professional life, gay executives have already crossed through the portal to a place where it's perfectly fine to *be thyself*. As a direct result, they believe in their own personal and professional value as a starting point for their roles as organizational leaders.

At the crux of these authentically led environments is trust. Without the trust of your employees, it's difficult if not impossible to develop an engaged and motivated workforce. For example, in my research, I found that gays and lesbians who were closeted in their professional lives were often locked out of the very workplace communication networks so critical to career success—the reason, for the most part, being that colleagues and supervisors just didn't know who they were.

Regardless of what is being kept hidden, whether it's sexual orientation or some other perceived disadvantage, the point is that you don't want someone on your team if you don't know who they are as an individual. Again, it's about trust. Because the gay executives profiled in this book have all found the freedom to incorporate their own authenticity into their professional roles, they enjoy a positive dynamic of trust that contributes to their ability to develop environments where employee engagement, job satisfaction, and workplace morale are comparatively impressive.

10

WHY MAKING A DIFFERENCE MAKES A DIFFERENCE

In many ways, G Quotient leadership is a direct reflection of Abraham Maslow's famous theory of the hierarchy of needs. In addition to physiological needs like food, water, and sleep, Maslow said, human beings need to feel safe, to belong, and be respected—by themselves as well as others. Finally, when all these needs have been met, Maslow believed, people are then able to realize their own potential as they pursue and achieve their dreams. Beginning with basic needs for survival and ending with self-actualization, Maslow's theory comprehensively represents how employment in G Quotient environments meets each of these levels of need for empowered employees. For the purposes of this discussion, consider that self-actualization can best be characterized by how employees feel about their work and themselves on the ride home at the end of the day. It's the feeling that their work makes a difference, and that they are appreciated and valued for their contributions.

Whatever the context of the workplace environment, from the Peace Corps to a Fortune 500 company, feeling and believing that the time invested in work makes a difference is one of the most significant and lasting effects of G Quotient leadership. Making a difference takes on two forms relative to G Quotient leadership. The first deals with how gay executives are making a difference in the lives of their employees. The second is about how, in turn, employees are making a difference in the lives of customers and clients through their work. In this context, G Quotient leadership is clearly what provides these employees with the type of meaning that motivates them to "make a difference" based on their own talents, skills, and initiative. Uniquely defined by each employee, making a difference in the lives of customers and clients ranges from manufacturing furniture that adds comfort and beauty to people's homes to advising corporations about how to succeed in the global marketplace.

G Quotient Employees

To understand how both of these forms of making a difference work together, it's vital to the scope of this book to represent the experiences of the people who work in these environments. The following ten interviews are examples of the positive impact that G Quotient leadership has on the lives and careers of employees who report to gay executives. Some interviews focus on specific principles, others speak to the effectiveness of G Quotient leadership as a complete paradigm. In several cases, I have included more than one employee from the same organization or working unit to provide greater perspective relative to that specific environment. I've selected these particular interviews because I feel they best represent the collective experience of the many employees who shared their insights with me during the course of my research. Over time, I will be making these additional interviews available on my Web site at www.kirksnyder.com and invite you to read more about employees who continue to benefit through G Quotient leadership.

Charley Holt
Director of Marketing
Mitchell Gold + Bob Williams

A straight man who reports to gay executives, Charley Holt grew up just thirty minutes away from what is now the company's headquarters in Taylorsville, North Carolina. At the beginning of our interview, Charley told me that like most people in this region of the country, he grew up thinking that being gay was just about the worst possible attribute you could attach to another human being.

In fact, when we began to discuss the subject, Charley was very careful in how he chose his words. As soon as I told him not to worry about political correctness, our exchange turned into one of the most profound interviews conducted for this book.

Before coming to work for Mitchell and Bob, Charley said, he didn't know anyone who was gay. The conservative social climate of this region means that very few people here openly identify as being gay. Therefore the opportunity for exposure to any type of positive gay diversity is almost nonexistent. Five years ago, when he started to work for the company, Charley honestly didn't know what to expect going to work for a "gay" company. "Who I am now," Charley said, "is very different from who I was then." He told me that getting to know Mitchell and Bob completely changed his preconceived ideas about gay people. Charley shared that he feels like more of a "complete person," because he now looks at the world from a much broader perspective. "I would say it's actually a more truthful point of view, because it's based on my own impressions and not outside influences."

Since joining Mitchell Gold + Bob Williams in a sales role, Charley said he has grown personally as well as professionally. Today, as director of marketing, he's responsible for national advertising campaigns as well as creative and media buying. He also oversees the consumer inquiry department, working with the company's public relations department. Along the way, Charley told me, the company has supported him in his role as a single father, providing him with the type of flexibility that adds value to his son's life as well as his own. He said, "Because my son is currently enrolled in the on-site day care at the Child Enrichment Center, I get to see him several times, every single day." Charley even told me that he had named his son after one of the company's famous lines of chairs.

This type of support also adds value to the workplace environment itself. When I asked Charley to describe the environment at Mitchell Gold + Bob Williams, he said, "Because of Mitchell and Bob, we don't feel the nine-to-five mentality that describes how a lot of people feel in other companies. There's much less separation between home and work, because 'work' isn't something to tolerate. In many ways it feels more like work, family, and playtime all at once, and that's a direct reflection of how Mitchell and Bob treat their employees. They treat people like family, and that's how we feel when we come to work." Charley said that all the accolades the company has received over the years about being a preferred employer definitely aren't public relations spin. "Mitchell and Bob really do care about the well-being of their employees and put their money where their mouth is. That's what makes it real. They walk the talk every day."

Amy Sullivan
Sales Support Manager
CitiCapital

Amy Sullivan has worked under Brent Mitchell's management since they both became part of CitiCapital in the 2000 acquisition I described earlier, in Brent's interview. Although they'd worked for the same company prior to the acquisition, Brent and Amy had been on opposite coasts and had never met prior to coming together in their new professional home at CitiCapital. Soon after we began our interview, Amy summed up her commitment to her boss with the following statement. She said, "Each time Brent gets promoted, I always request to move with him."

According to Amy, one of the reasons why she is so committed to Brent is that he has become a positive part of her own career path. "He encourages me to drive my career in a forward direction, and gets me involved in those areas that will help me reach my goals."

I asked Amy how Brent's leadership differed from other managers she's worked for in the past, and whether or not it made an impact on her life beyond the workplace. Her answer reminded me of a point Mitchell Gold and Bob Williams emphasized in their interview—that inclusion is about *all* types of demographics. For Amy, this includes being a working mother. On this subject, Amy said that she's all too aware of the stereotypes often associated with working mothers. "Personally, some of the stereotypes I've encountered include the false idea that working mothers don't really *want* to work. Or that we won't work as hard as people without children. No matter what it is, they're all focused on the negative instead of the positive." I asked her if being a working mother has had a negative impact on her current job? "Those types of thoughts simply don't exist for Brent. I've honestly never felt judged or looked down on because I'm a working mom. Instead, I feel supported and encouraged to do those things in my personal life that, I can absolutely tell you, make me a better employee. Brent respects people as individuals and doesn't buy into stereotypes. It's one of his strengths as a manager."

Citing a recent example, Amy told me that she needed to leave work early one day a week for several weeks to attend a mother-daughter dance class. I was struck by her use of the word *empower*. "Brent empowers me to make these types of decisions on my own. He knew this class was a big deal to me, and as an employee, trusted me to get my job done." She said, "Instead of going home with negative feelings, thinking, 'my job is causing me to miss out on an important part of my life,' I go home with a positive attitude and an even stronger desire to do a really good job for him." At the end of our interview, I asked Amy how Brent's leadership has made a difference in her own level of engagement. "Brent's respect and trust is what makes a difference. It inspires me to be successful at work." After a brief pause, she added, "It makes me want *all* of us to succeed."

Christopher Newman and Carolyn Stirling
Admissions Counselors
USC Rossier School of Education

As part of Kevin Colaner's team, both Christopher and Carolyn guide prospective students through the admissions and enrollment process, representing the School of Education all over the country. Reporting to Kevin for almost two years, Christopher said that prior to working at USC, he was the only African American male in an office of twelve, ten of whom were white women. Comparing the two settings, he told me that his old organizational culture felt like it was structured in a way that encouraged employees to work in isolation. "My supervisor seemed bothered if I knocked on the door and asked a question. As a result, I felt a strong sense of disconnection, which very often limited my ability to be as effective as I could have been in an environment that was team-oriented." Christopher said the environment at Rossier is 180 degrees opposite. "Kevin is very honest; he will give you the good with the bad, and I never have to translate a covert agenda." It's a dynamic that Christopher said began on his first day. "Kevin shared a story with me about his 'conservative' parents. During the conversation, without missing a beat, he said, 'Oh, by the way, I'm gay.' As a straight male, I thought, 'If he can be that open with me then I will be able to be open with him.'" Christopher said that he believes this kind of honesty has built a supportive workplace environment where teamwork and collaboration are daily occurrences.

Carolyn echoes Christopher's sentiment on teamwork and collaboration: "Kevin is very team-oriented and encourages the professional development of each member of our team. It's a real luxury to work in an environment where you know you are supported." Carolyn also touched on a point that speaks directly to why personal value will continue to matter in the workplace. It goes back to a premise highlighted throughout this book: G Quotient leaders motivate instead of dictate. On this subject, Carolyn said, "When you work with Kevin, he makes you feel like you work *with* him, not *for* him. He gives you the tools and space to excel and supports you all the way. It makes such a difference to feel like what you do matters."

Toby Pearlstein and Barbara Bilodeau
Director of Global Information Services;
Director of Market Research & Analysis
Bain & Company

Because Steven Tallman's interview focused on the G Quotient principle of creativity, I wanted to hear how two of his direct reports felt about his leadership relative to this topic.

Addressing the value of creativity as a principle of Steven's leadership, Toby presented a cause-and-effect scenario. "Since our firm itself is diverse and inclusive, it has allowed Steven to build on these values in his own organization. In this respect, it fosters a culture of respect for all points of view, which is very helpful in pushing us to think creatively." As part of the administrative department, Toby said, he sees the type of mutual respect promoted through Steven's leadership resulting in a much greater integration with the consulting side of the company.

Toby also talked about Steven's creativity in the context of how it has led the organization to be more competitive in a changing world. "There have been sea changes related to the provision of external information services over the past few years. Steven has always been forward thinking in how these changes can be seen as opportunities for how Information Services can further Bain's mission as well as our organization's consulting staff on a day-to-day basis." Because creativity leads to innovation, which in turn creates the need for adaptability to change, these examples speak to the effectiveness with which G Quotient leadership goes beyond the immediate environment to enhance the success of the greater organization.

Barbara said that Steven often uses creativity to provide the firm with a competitive advantage. "Steven's strengths are that he is incredibly creative and sees connections between things that others might miss. If he becomes aware of a problem, he quickly comes up with possible solutions and is very good at then working with colleagues across the firm to evaluate which is the best solution [to the problem]. Overall, he has the rare combination of developing good ideas, determining how to implement them, and finally, being able to convince others why they should become invested in the ideas themselves."

Jack Whitley and Andrew Spainhour
Vice President of Internet Sales & Marketing;
General Counsel
Replacements, Ltd.

Both Jack Whitley and Andrew Spainhour report directly to Replacements' president and founder, Bob Page. Both told me that working with Bob over the years has taught them about the positive impact that can be made when organizational leaders place great value on people and their ideas. They both agree that at Replacements, it's been an ongoing source of business success.

When Jack began working for Bob in 1993, sales were between $18 million and $20 million. Today, with sales of more than $70 million, Jack told me that he's been fortunate to be part of a company that has more than tripled its earnings, because it's equipped him with firsthand knowledge about what it takes to grow success over time. Jack said that there is also an "intellectual curiosity and a quest for excellence" about Bob that encourages his employees to have the freedom to propose new ideas. Jack said that one of the biggest lessons he has learned from working with Bob was to commit to "thinking young." He said, "Bob is always enthusiastic about looking at the horizon regarding what might be out there next. He has the courage to take risks and follow through on his intuition. I've worked to incorporate this approach into my own management and leadership style, because it's made a big difference in the quality of my own work life. It enhances motivation and gets you involved in the organization."

One of the first questions I asked Jack was about his perspective on Bob's stated belief in adaptability as a principle of his leadership. I was curious to see if he felt it had enhanced his own professional experience in the organization. According to Jack, "Because Bob isn't afraid of change, it enables him to be open to new ideas and different ways of thinking that benefits the company. In my thirteen years with Replacements, no matter how busy Bob has been at the time, he's always been willing to listen to my ideas. Speaking for myself, this kind of openness is more than motivating. It's energizing."

One of the interesting things that Jack shared with me directly reflects what many gay executives said about giving honest feedback. It's a reminder that G Quotient leadership isn't about false enthusiasm or insincere opinions. Jack said that when you pitch an idea to Bob, one of the most valuable outcomes is that there will always be an "honest and open discussion about the chances for the proposed idea to succeed." Jack said that he believes that this type of "authentic response" has been a key to Bob's success as a leader.

Andrew Spainhour, Bob's general counsel, said, "Working for Bob is an adventure." He told me that Bob embraces change in ways that very few other people do. "He is a visionary entrepreneur, and his mind works in a way that mine simply does not. I feel that I am constantly learning from Bob, and as someone who aspires to be a lifelong learner, that means a great deal to me." When I asked Andrew what lesson he feels has made the most impact on his own beliefs about leadership, he offered a very candid response. "I think we corporate lawyers often find ourselves in a responsive or reactive posture, given how much there is for us to do. Working for Bob and for Replacements has simply forced me to see change as a bedrock business principle."

Andrew said that because the company is constantly evolving, as the company leader, Bob drives change to an extraordinary degree. As a result, Andrew said, "I've learned that it's essential to anticipate change and to stay ahead of it. Doing so gives us the opportunity to prepare on the front end for any type of change that might impact the company so we can make the best possible decisions for the health of the business."

Kelly M. Smith
Chief Financial Officer
Replacements, Ltd.

As CFO, Kelly has the job of advising and reporting on the financial health of the business. When I asked Kelly to describe how Bob's leadership has made a difference in the quality of his own professional life, he gave me a truly great sound bite: "Complacency is so easy and change is so hard. Bob has helped instill in all of us the importance of choosing the right path even if it's the harder path, in order to improve the organization." In this respect, Kelly said, this kind of adaptability is not just something Bob expects of others.

"Bob leads by example and isn't afraid to choose a more difficult path for himself if he believes it's the right one." Kelly told me that seeing Bob hold the bar higher for himself inspires him to hold the bar higher as well. "I know I'm a better leader in my own right for having worked in Bob's organization. I never again want to work where the status quo is good enough; working with Bob helps you to see new possibilities every day."

Rita Stockett
Director of Product Innovation
PepsiCo

According to Rita Stockett, Steve Sears strikes an effective balance between involvement and empowerment. "Steve is very balanced in his approach to management, which is inspiring. He's there when he is needed, but lets his employees do their job. That kind of trust makes a big difference when it comes to being fully committed to your work."

Rita said that Steve is the only manager she has worked for where she has given her all because she wanted to as opposed to being pushed into engagement. "Even though I've always been committed to professional achievement throughout my career, at times it's been difficult to maintain that commitment at a personal level. As an African American woman, I haven't always felt each of my managers has made inclusion a priority. But with Steve it's just the opposite. His employees know they are valued." When I asked her how that impacts the day-to-day employee experience in the organization, she said, "It makes you want to give your all to the organization every day, because you know that your achievement depends on your abilities and not the color of your skin."

In Steve's organization, Rita told me, the expectation to job excellence is certainly a part of the environment, but he doesn't have to demand it. Steve gets this result by facilitating the processes of work instead of commanding an outcome. "He's very comfortable in sharing the spotlight and giving credit where credit is due. For me personally, this makes a big difference because it's about being appreciated. When you know you'll be recognized for your contributions, it gives you more incentive to make an impact."

From the very beginning of our interview, it was clear that Rita is someone who is committed to exceptional job performance. We talked about how being part of a minority population can sometimes increase the drive for professional excellence. "I think Steve and I share that commitment because we both understand that we're often scrutinized to a greater degree because of who we are as people. Unfortunately, some people may form opinions about an entire group of individuals based on the personal actions of one person— for better or worse. That's why I often feel a sense of responsibility to stand out."

Rita said that because Steve understands what this sense of responsibility feels like, he therefore recognizes the importance of creating an environment where diversity is not just something talked about as being valuable but is actually a factor in the organization's success. "Steve's approach to leadership authentically reflects the value of diversity, because he demonstrates an honest respect for all members of his team."

The Need for Challenge and Responsibility

For today's employees, in addition to making a difference, the need for challenge and responsibility has become a primary factor in engagement, satisfaction, and workplace morale. In G Quotient environments, gay executives address this need in part by trusting their employees to do their jobs. In *Rise of the Creative Class*, Richard Florida analyzed several statistical studies, including mountains of surveys from *Information Week* (in addition to his own research), to address the top ten motivational factors for workers in the information technology field. What he found was that *challenge* and *responsibility*, which he defines as "being able to contribute and have impact: knowing that one's work makes a difference," was the most important motivational factor in the workplace.[1]

I believe these defined motivational factors of IT workers play a key role in better understanding G Quotient leadership, because, quite simply, IT workers were the first wave of empowered employees. While the rest of us were still figuring out exactly what the Internet was capable of doing, IT workers were already clicking through it like pros. They were among the very first employees to collect industry-specific knowledge and share it with their equally as connected colleagues. In fact, if you were creating a time line for employee empowerment, these savvy professionals would appear at a very early point. It's exactly why companies at the height of the dot-com boom eliminated many of their existing policies for their IT employees, relaxing everything from dress codes to working schedules. Employers recognized that IT workers needed to be treated with individual respect and value, and adapted to these needs by creating what could arguably be defined as organizational subcultures of *inclusion*. It's a dynamic that is now repeating in G Quotient environments under the management of gay executives across all four sectors that I studied.

To continue with this line of thinking, with IT workers serving as an early representation of the needs and values of empowered employees, challenge and responsibility are destined to be top motivational factors for all twenty-first-century employees. If this is the case, then setting goals, treating employees fairly, and creating a workplace that addresses the needs of all employees as individuals will provide the canvas for creating organizations that supply these two motivational factors. As a group, gay executives realize that employee meaning drives organizational accomplishment, ultimately a primary force behind all definitions of motivation.

11

WHY G QUOTIENT LEADERSHIP CREATES A TWENTY-FIRST-CENTURY ADVANTAGE

The seven principles of G Quotient leadership will continue to matter in the new world of work because the underlying factors contributing to the reconstruction of contemporary employees are becoming more pervasive day by day. All the technologies that have contributed to employees' ability to throw back the corporate veil and see their employers in the often-harsh light of day are being accelerated at warp speed. It's why employees are reacting so vehemently when management tries to dictate their behavior. You simply can't dictate to someone who is highly knowledgeable, connected, and, as a result, empowered without eliciting a negative response. According to a 2005 article in *Communication World*, "Organizations that had counted on the lack of person-to-person communication to contain potentially damaging information suddenly found there were no secrets anymore."[1]

Among contemporary employees, even if the job doesn't require Internet access on the desktop, it's increasingly likely that they have access at home. In 2005, the Internet as a source of information in the United States was reported to be pervasive in more than 70 percent of total households. Worldwide, Internet users reached the one billion mark in 2005, with a five-year growth rate of more than 150 percent.[2] And I'm not just talking dial-up access, either. According to the annual study of Internet trends conducted by global survey-based marketing research firm Ipsos-Insight in its "Face of the Web" survey, high-speed broadband access reached 62 percent of those nearly one billion global Internet users in March 2005, up 24 percent over the previous year. In the United

States alone, Nielsen/NetRatings reported, high-speed home Internet access will exceed 70 percent (among Internet users) in 2006.[3] What this means is that we are not just connecting, we're connecting faster, better, and in a more omnipresent fashion than ever before.

As a result, we're also demanding and receiving more personalized and customized digital content (knowledge) across virtually all types of media. From television and computers to cell phones, iPods, and BlackBerrys, we are taking our tools for empowerment wherever we go. Built around personal interests, this phenomenon of customized digital content is reshaping how we live in the world because it's providing us with greater authority over our time and unique preferences. It's also merging content across different types of media, allowing us to interface with knowledge whenever and wherever we see fit. For example, according to the Internet research firm eMarketer, the number of U.S. consumers who will watch television programming on their mobile phones will rise to 15 million by 2009, up from just 1.2 million in 2005.[4]

In a related trend, consider that in 2004, approximately a million people in the United States had downloaded a podcast. By 2010, the number of people who will use a podcast to get information is predicted to rise to 63 million.[5] What's a podcast? The term refers to media files placed on Web sites and made available to the general public 24/7. Unlike media broadcasting live over the Internet, podcasts (which can also include photo images and text) are always there ready to be accessed. And it isn't just for techies. In March 2005, John Edwards became the first major U.S. politician to launch his own series of podcasts on a variety of subjects through his organization One America. This is just another example of how we will continue to expand our knowledge-base over the next decade—again, on our own terms and conditions.

All these documented trends account for the knowledge and interconnectivity factors in the employee empowerment equation. And this interconnectivity is also poised to accelerate to new levels. According to Yahoo!, a growing number of people are already getting used to the delivery of personalized content via a type of technology called RSS, which in one widely used translation means "Really Simple Syndication." Thousands of Web sites are now using this technology to distribute new content that has been added to their site according to individual interests. While RSS is for the time being primarily focused on news, it can be customized to include other types of subject matter, including specialized information about specific fields and industries. When it's received, people are encouraged by the sender to pass it along to friends, family, and coworkers who may share an interest in the same information. In this sense, everyone will conceivably have the potential to become a news provider, furthering the trend of employee empowerment across the globe.

G Quotient Leadership and Globalization

Globalization is widely used as a term to describe the impact on nations resulting from both world trade and cultural exchange. While the concept of globalization has been around as long as there have been modes of transportation, life in the Digital Age has changed its context. More than ever before, people from around the world have seemingly infinite opportunities to become instantly informed about the unique characteristics that make up different societies. However, globalization in today's context calls on business leaders to do more than understand these differences. There's a secondary need to adapt to the multicultural diversity that results from economic interdependence.

Because economic interdependence requires the reduction of social barriers as well as political barriers in order to flourish, being able to demonstrate mutual respect and tolerance for cultural diversity is critical to the success of global business leadership. It's akin to what many employees reporting to gay executives identified as "walking the talk": in this case, adapting to multicultural diversity rather than just understanding it—a precept that gay executives appear to be embracing through the principles of G Quotient leadership.

With the realities of globalization now looking U.S. business leaders square in the face, it's no longer possible to put off dealing with how diversity affects the day-to-day activities of all types of organizations. According to John Challenger, CEO of international outplacement consulting firm Challenger, Gray & Christmas, "We must rally our companies, schools, and country to embrace diversity." Challenger states that as a country, we have to "broaden and deepen our language skills, encourage international studies and travel, and reach out and engage other cultures." He also says there is no room for "ugly Americans" on the global stage.[6]

A 2005 article in *Chief Executive,* reporting on the sixth annual CEO leadership summit that took place in Palm Beach, Florida, says that the U.S. economy is at a historic crossroads. Whether or not the United States gains strength or loses its comparative advantage will depend on how it handles this new context of globalization while being able to innovate and adapt. According to Fred Smith, CEO of FedEx, "The manufacturing base is migrating away from the United States." Citing the pressure being exerted most prominently by China, Smith said, "I think the difference between the Chinese and any other economy that we've faced since the end of World War II is that they are entrepreneurial in nature."[7] Both China and India have a tremendous resource of well-trained and educated workers who are ready, willing, and able to go to work for U.S. companies for a fraction of the cost of U.S. workers. A January 2006 Reuters report on the global economy indicated that while U.S. manufacturing posted slower growth, Asian and euro zone counterparts continued to make further improvements.[8]

Without a workforce that is engaged, satisfied, and happy in its environment, remaining competitive at global levels is at best, going to be a struggle over the next ten years. Beginning with the G Quotient leadership principle of inclusion and continuing on through creativity, adaptability, connection, communication, intuition, and collaboration, the beliefs and behaviors behind G Quotient leadership are an exact match for both understanding and adapting to the issues of globalization in today's business landscape.

Specifically, the global demands of twenty-first-century leadership are most notably represented in the G Quotient principles of inclusion, communication, and connectivity. As a trio, they collectively symbolize the philosophies and sensitivities necessary to capitalize on the business as well as social integration associated with an interdependent global economy.

Throughout my research for this book, I found a strong sense among gay executives that their workplace actions have an impact on the world beyond their immediate environments. Along with this awareness, I also found a shared feeling of what might best be described as *leadership responsibility*. The most apparent manifestation of having a global perspective of leadership was summed up by one executive as being a significant motivating force behind his own approach to leadership. He said, "Because I believe what I say and do may wind up making an impact on someone's life on the other side of the world, I feel a tremendous obligation to be as thoughtful as possible—even when making the smallest of business decisions." It's part of a greater perspective that looks at life in *us* terms as opposed to *me* terms, a widely held ideal among gay men that goes back to the issues of community development discussed earlier in this book.

As business leaders, gay men have developed a professional mind-set that assumes that power and success are meant to be shared and not something to be held by only a few. Further, by demonstrating respect and value for others through their leadership, they act on a conscious belief that new alliances and partnerships will grow out of these behaviors, further contributing to greater balance and opportunities for all types of people—in their own backyards as well as around the globe.

Generation Y

Generation Y is different. As a group, Gen Y is estimated to begin somewhere between 1978 and 1982, and end between 1995 and 2000. Seventy million strong, it is about to make a mighty impact on the workplace. I've taught and advised members of Gen Y for the better part of the last ten years at the university level, so I feel I can speak about them, although certainly not for them, with some degree of authority. Granted, USC is a large urban campus in Los Angeles, and it thus represents a different type of student population from what you'd find on a conservative campus in the Bible belt. However, regardless of where Gen Y members may actually live or go to school, their views and values are for the most part shaped by many of the same influences because they are all pervasively connected—to each other and to the world at large.

In *Employing Generation Why*, noted Gen Y expert Eric Chester writes, "Generation Y has never known life without cell phones, pagers, fax machines, and voice mail. Their world has always included minivans, bottled water, cable television, overnight package delivery, and chat rooms."[9] In addition, their world has also included globalization, corporate scandals, and an all-encompassing media presence.

As a result of all of the information they have had access to throughout their lives, Gen Y consists of extremely knowledgeable and empowered young people who are going to continue the transformation currently under way in the world of work. Collectively, they have few doubts about their own potential and abilities, something I admire a great deal.

In a 2005 article in *USA Today* titled "Generation Y: They've Arrived at Work with a New Attitude," Gen Y workers are described as having high expectations for themselves, high expectations of what their employers should provide them, and a need for creative challenges to stay engaged in their work. They also view their colleagues as vast professional resources.[10] This is a very specific set of beliefs and behaviors that directly reflect the beliefs and behaviors associated with G Quotient leadership.

In research conducted by RainmakerThinking, a U.S. research and consulting firm that specializes in studying the working lives of young people, the firm's founder, Bruce Tulgan, reports that Gen Y expects managers to take an active role in employees' professional development. The firm's research identifies the top three job requirements for members of Gen Y in the following order:[11]

1. Meaningful work that makes a difference to the world.
2. Working with committed coworkers who share their values.
3. Meeting their own personal goals.

Jordan Kaplan, an associate professor of management science at Long Island University-Brooklyn, is quoted as saying, "They've grown up questioning their parents, and now they're questioning their employers. They don't know how to shut up, which is great, but that's aggravating to the 50-year-old manager who says, 'Do it and do it now.'"[12]

The members of Gen Y are entering the workforce as empowered employees. As products of the Digital Age, they grew up on a diet of instant access to specialized knowledge and are interconnected in a way that is simply an extension of their everyday life. Connection, to both information and people, is second nature. The professional expectations of Gen Y are not unique to the United States. These same influences represent a global impact. For example, in the United Kingdom, it's estimated that up to half of Gen Y employees recruited into companies via college recruiting programs will leave within two years. In a study conducted by Siemens, one of the world's largest electrical engineering and electronics companies and headquartered in Berlin and Munich, in cooperation with The Work Foundation, researchers found that the U.K. retention problem "was not about money, but about understanding their views and needs." The study found that to retain Gen Y talent, companies will have to work harder to establish a common language.[13]

At a 2004 speakers forum at MIT called "Changing Media, Changing Audiences," Betsy Frank, executive vice president for research and planning at MTV Networks identified diversity among the key factors that influence the viewing patterns of Gen Y. She said that this generation actively seeks out programming with diversity, which accounts for the enormous popularity of cable programs on MTV Networks that feature a variety of demographic types. Among Gen Y viewers, there was greater comfort in talking about race, ethnicity, and sexual orientation.[14]

Social values are shaped by the prevailing worldview we develop throughout a lifetime of experiences. When the context of life changes, social values are subject to change as well. It's one of the reasons why coming out of the closet has had such a significant impact on how gay executives approach business leadership. For example, when authenticity becomes a major component of how a leader approaches life, it makes an impact on subsequent interactions with employees. One of the greatest differences between Gen Y and earlier generations is reflected in how they view society and traditional social values. In terms of the workplace, their own worldview will make a significant impact on how they believe organizations should be managed. Greenberg Quinlan Rosner, one of the world's premier research and strategic consulting firms, reported in 2005 that 57 percent of Gen Y believes that the institution of marriage is dying in the United States. The report states that only half of these young people agree that marriage is one of the most important institutions in American society. Based on these views, it's no surprise that they offer less critical judgments on the subject of gay marriage. A 58 percent majority of Gen Y supports gay marriage, a stark contrast to other demographic populations when segmented solely based on age.[15] The report also found that support for gay marriage increases in correlation with the number of gay or lesbian friends and associates these young people have in their own lives, with 82 percent reporting that they know at least one gay individual and a third reporting they have a close friend who is gay or lesbian. This less judgmental and more tolerant outlook is further evidence that Gen Y will be much more inclusive business leaders than previous generations, the hallmark of G Quotient leadership.

The annual CIRP survey, sponsored by the Higher Education Research Institute and the Cooperative Institutional Research Program, collects information about the educational goals, values, and attitudes on a variety of social issues among nearly three hundred thousand entering college freshman in the United States. Among the projected graduating class of 2008, 41 percent report that becoming successful in their own business is either essential or highly important in their professional lives.[16] This value for independence will arguably play a prime role in their approach to management in existing organizations as well as in those they start on their own. As one of the ten things every manager needs to know about G Quotient leadership, the sense of entrepreneurship fostered by gay executives within their organizations appears to be in synch with the values of Gen Y. Like gay executives who are out of the closet and succeeding in their own skin, members of Gen Y similarly feel empowered to achieve relative to their own individuality. With this influx of people who are self-governing, self-determined, and driven to "be the best" independent of external coercion, the influence of autonomy within organizations worldwide is presumably going to get stronger.

I am convinced that Gen Y will be tenacious achievers at a global level because they are extremely accepting of the ideals behind multiculturalism. They are not afraid of hard work either in the classroom or in the workplace, and I have found them to have an extremely positive outlook about how they can make a difference in the world—not dissimilar to the gay executives profiled in this book. It's why the seven principles of G Quotient leadership are well positioned to increase in value over time.

The Shift to a New Era of Leadership

Traditional leadership paradigms were born out of a hierarchal society where men, presumably straight and predominantly white, possessed the most power. Because traditional society also cast these men in the role of breadwinner, the world of work has historically centered around their beliefs and behaviors. Today, in a diverse world that is increasingly more horizontal, traditional leadership paradigms centered on one central figure are no longer effective because power and therefore success are becoming more equally distributed. This is why the G Quotient theme of balance is meeting with such widespread approval in the recalibrated workplace. As discussed throughout this book, empowered employees need to be heard.

The shift toward a more horizontal business playing field is also making an impact on the very definition of *manager* and *leader*. Traditional experts have typically separated managers and leaders into two distinct organizational functions. Good managers have been defined as being highly efficient decision makers, charged with keeping a watchful eye over budgets while making sure that the immediate goals of the organization are being met. Good leaders, on the other hand, have been defined more as visionaries, setting the overall course of the organization with a greater focus on long-term success.

With the shift away from pyramid-shaped hierarchies, it's no longer prudent to separate these two functions. Quite simply, employees have evolved to the point where job engagement and a commitment to professional excellence must be based on the recognition of their individual value rather than as a by-product of direct supervision. To accomplish this, companies must include their employees in the visionary process. This type of integration is impossible to achieve if employees are several organizational layers away from where that function takes place. G Quotient leadership brings this function to the front line of organizations and engages employees in their jobs by making them part of the organization's future—motivating them through involvement and inclusion rather than dictating their behavior purely through the function of management. Once the primary tool for employee engagement in a hierarchal society, the command and control of job performance has become outdated baggage as we move forward into a world of work that has a more equitable power structure. Ken Blanchard once said, "None of us is as smart as all of us." That belief reverberates throughout all aspects of G Quotient leadership.

I offer students the following analogy for thinking about balance within organizations. If you imagine the workplace as the framework for a generic A-frame building, consider that the pillars of the building represent the workforce and the roofline symbolizes the organization itself, including its leadership. Like any structure, without pillars in place for support, the roofline will collapse and the building or organization will subsequently implode. I always make sure to emphasize that this analogy isn't about employees being able to hold leadership hostage and take over the company. Instead, it represents an organizational point of view that recognizes employees as being central to success, highly illustrative of the recalibration that has taken place across all fields and industries in the new world of work.

As noted in this book's Introduction, gay men have been documented leaders across the centuries in nearly all fields except business. Until recently, finding success as a non-closeted gay business leader was out of the question because the confines of a traditional society didn't provide that type of professional access. Today, based on the set of beliefs and behaviors described throughout this book as G Quotient leadership, gay executives and entrepreneurs in widely disparate fields and industries are experiencing record levels of success as *leaders* of their own respective organizations. At the same time, their careers are flourishing.

G Quotient leadership is ultimately about the empowerment of anyone seeking to advance as an organizational leader in the recalibrated workplace—including *all* business professionals regardless of age, ethnicity, gender, or sexual orientation. When equipped with a better understanding of the needs and expectations of today's employees, every manager can gain the insight necessary to fully engage the talents and skills of what is easily the most sophisticated workforce in history. More knowledgeable and empowered than ever imagined, today's employees have the ability to take us beyond the Digital Age into whatever defines the next frontier. G Quotient leadership provides a framework for success that every manager can use to become the leader everyone wants to work for—and the leader everyone wants to hire.

APPENDIX A

WHAT'S YOUR GQ?

The G Quotient Assessment

As a human activity, leadership is highly reflective of individual beliefs and behaviors. This appendix presents an assessment tool designed to provide additional insight about how the management-based beliefs and behaviors of individuals and groups align with the principles of G Quotient leadership.

Like other such instruments, including the Myers-Briggs Type Indicator (MBTI), the G Quotient Assessment is an *assessment* rather than a *test*, because it has no right or wrong answers. Therefore, the goal in taking it isn't to score higher than a friend or colleague. Rather, it's simply one of many ways to gain insight about how you approach leadership, something to use as a tool for educational and professional development.

Background

There are several ways that researchers build assessment tools to measure beliefs and behaviors. One way is to collect information from individual responses to different situations based on vignettes or case studies. This requires people to read about and become familiar with particular scenarios, and then answer questions about how they would respond in the given circumstance. Another popular method is to collect samples of responses to statements concerning the beliefs and behaviors under investigation, and then analyze the results so as to produce a measure (a score). This is an approach that requires statistically evaluating the character of the statements for internal consistency as well as utility in assessing the area of interest (in this case, G Quotient leadership). The latter method was how the G Quotient assessment was developed (the descriptive statistics are detailed in Appendix C).

The development and validation of a new assessment instrument requires a specialized area of psychological and psychometric education and experience. It's one that certainly falls outside my own area of expertise. Having gone through an intensive training program to become certified in the MBTI, I have a great appreciation and respect for the professionals who develop and validate these types of assessments. Without question, it's an art that calls on both creative and linear talents and skills.

I therefore enlisted the aid of Mark S. Majors, a renowned counseling psychologist with extensive psychometric experience, to help develop the G Quotient assessment and validate the statistics. In addition to developing the MajorsPTI (which identifies psychological type), he was a principal data analyst on the 1994 Strong Interest Inventory, the MBTI Form M, and a developer and manual coauthor for the new MBTI Form Q.

Our first step was to develop a questionnaire that captured the collective meaning of G Quotient leadership. The initial data collection was based on a fifty-two-statement version of the instrument. Responses were collected from 220 managers—gay and straight, male and female—addressing their beliefs and behaviors relative to the seven G Quotient principles.

For any assessment to be valid, there must be a measured consistency in how people respond to similar types of statements. In this sense, the question is not whether people actually respond to the statements in terms of assigning a rating. Instead, it's whether they respond to the same types of statements in a consistent manner. That's what gives consistent meaning and support for validity to all types of measured assessments. Then, based on these findings, certain statements found to be less consistent are weeded out and the final assessment is developed. The final version of the G Quotient assessment contains twenty-five statements.

Through the development and validation process, the collected information also provided an opportunity to evaluate and compare the content of these responses as the final phase of research. Many of these statistics are presented throughout this book and identified through footnotes.

The G Quotient assessment appears in full here because I believe it is important to explain what G Quotient leadership is all about so every manager can understand the utility of the assessment. Of course, a high or low score in no way has any bearing on an individual's sexual orientation. In fact, we saw a healthy range of scores within each demographic group, suggesting that, as already stated, the G Quotient is not an exclusively gay management style—it is an approach to leadership that is making a positive impact in the recalibrated world of work.

The G Quotient Assessment

For each of the following twenty-five statements, select and circle one rating response that best describes your beliefs and behaviors. (Ignore the fill-in lines that precede each item; they're for use in the scoring process after the assessment is complete.) As with all assessments, the utility of the G Quotient Assessment is dependent upon truthful responses. Try not to spend too much time analyzing each statement or trying to determine which rating will result in the highest GQ score. Typically your first response will be the most accurate.

Note: A scoring key follows the assessment.

_____   1. I do not believe that my organization or business can reach full potential without the input and participation of all employees.

Never   Seldom   Sometimes   Frequently   Always

_____ 2. A key to my management style is discerning my employees' motivational pathways.

Never   Seldom   Sometimes   Frequently   Always

_____ 3. I depend upon my employees for new ways of accomplishing tasks and meeting goals.

Never   Seldom   Sometimes   Frequently   Always

_____ 4. I believe that changing the organization or business environment to help employees with the practical aspects of life is critical.

Never   Seldom   Sometimes   Frequently   Always

_____ 5. I don't get much back from the energy that I put into professional relationships.

Never   Seldom   Sometimes   Frequently   Always

_____ 6. My actions to facilitate an employee's growth and development improve the work environment.

Never   Seldom   Sometimes   Frequently   Always

_____ 7. The contacts that I have with others in leadership roles facilitate my success.

Never   Seldom   Sometimes   Frequently   Always

_____ 8. My role as manager or supervisor, while important, is not superior in value to the roles of those in my employ.

Never   Seldom   Sometimes   Frequently   Always

_____ 9. I rely upon brainstorming with my employees for new concepts that give our organization or business the edge.

Never   Seldom   Sometimes   Frequently   Always

_____ 10. Losing a good employee to a promotion is frequently detrimental to the organization or business financially, as well as a drain on my energy.

Never   Seldom   Sometimes   Frequently   Always

_____ 11. I believe it is important to be able to recognize and make use of the talents my employees have.

Never   Seldom   Sometimes   Frequently   Always

_____ 12. It is important to me that all my employees know that I value and respect them all equally well.

Never   Seldom   Sometimes   Frequently   Always

_____ 13. I have discovered that when the process of working together is enjoyable, the work gets done.

Never   Seldom   Sometimes   Frequently   Always

_____ 14. I enjoy keeping my organization or business on the move and adapting to the times.

Never   Seldom   Sometimes   Frequently   Always

_____ 15. Too much energy is spent adapting to changes in my organization or business that can be done without.

Never   Seldom   Sometimes   Frequently   Always

_____ 16. I find that diverse populations result in diverse talents and skills, all of which are important for the success of my organization or business.

Never   Seldom   Sometimes   Frequently   Always

_____ 17. When things are not going well in my organization or business, I look for organizational failures rather than individual failures.

Never   Seldom   Sometimes   Frequently   Always

_____ 18. When my employees contribute to the innovation within the organization or business, they feel connected and valued.

Never   Seldom   Sometimes   Frequently   Always

_____ 19. I find that I am able to spot a good deal without necessarily hearing all the facts.

Never   Seldom   Sometimes   Frequently   Always

_____ 20. It is important not to lean upon hunches as a manager but trust only in the facts.

Never Seldom Sometimes Frequently Always

_____ 21. My ability to bring out the best in my employees comes from my ability to see and understand their needs and wants.

Never Seldom Sometimes Frequently Always

_____ 22. As a manager I have a knack for putting people together in ways that result in successful working relationships.

Never Seldom Sometimes Frequently Always

_____ 23. I want to see all employees aspire to and attain higher positions.

Never Seldom Sometimes Frequently Always

_____ 24. Justice and equity in the treatment of employees is one of my basic rules.

Never Seldom Sometimes Frequently Always

_____ 25. I believe that my organization or business runs smoothest using tried-and-true processes and procedures.

Never Seldom Sometimes Frequently Always

Scoring Key

For each of the designated statements, use the following table to assign a numerical score that corresponds to your answer, then add everything to obtain a final score.

Statements 1–4:   Never = 1; Seldom = 2; Sometimes = 3; Frequently = 4; Always = 5

Statement 5:   Never = 5; Seldom = 4; Sometimes = 3; Frequently = 2; Always = 1

Statements 6–9:	Never = 1; Seldom = 2; Sometimes = 3; Frequently = 4; Always = 5
Statement 10:	Never = 5; Seldom = 4; Sometimes = 3; Frequently = 2; Always = 1
Statements 11–14:	Never = 1; Seldom = 2; Sometimes = 3; Frequently = 4; Always = 5
Statement 15:	Never = 5; Seldom = 4; Sometimes = 3; Frequently = 2; Always = 1
Statements 16–19:	Never = 1; Seldom = 2; Sometimes = 3; Frequently = 4; Always = 5
Statement 20:	Never = 5; Seldom = 4; Sometimes = 3; Frequently = 2; Always = 1
Statements 21–24:	Never = 1; Seldom = 2; Sometimes = 3; Frequently = 4; Always = 5
Statement 25:	Never = 5; Seldom = 4; Sometimes = 3; Frequently = 2; Always = 1

Interpreting your GQ

The range of possible GQ scores is 25–125. Among the research group of 220 managers, the average score for the 116 gay managers was 110.50 with a range of 61–124. Because gay men are the first group of managers identified to widely practice G Quotient leadership, as a collective population, they represent nearly 53 percent of this segment of the research.

Of course, the first thing everyone wants to know is how their score compares with other demographic populations: gay men, lesbians, straight women, and straight men. Critical to the purpose of this as well as other assessments is to reiterate that scores are simply one piece of the information puzzle. In this sense, no assessment is capable of determining all the beliefs and behaviors of any individual or population. With that said, the average GQ scores for the four populations are as follows:

Population	Average	Range
Gay Men	110.50	61–124
Lesbians	101.67	74–123
Straight Women	93.25	68–116
Straight Men	80.02	61–119

As stated, one of the most notable findings is the range of scores within each population. While gay men did have the highest average score, these ranges suggest that the beliefs and behaviors associated with G Quotient leadership can be identified in all four measured populations. Appendix C breaks down how each population responded to the twenty-five statements in percentages. Among gay men, I found a distinction in three key areas, which contributed to an overall higher average GQ score. These distinctions call on the same three fundamental skills earlier identified as being prevalent strengths among gay men, namely adaptability, intuitive communication, and creative problem solving.

APPENDIX B

RESEARCH OVERVIEW

Developed over a period of five years, the research for *The G Quotient* spans more than 3,000 working professionals, representing diverse organizations across the fields of business, education, government and nonprofit, and independent entrepreneurial enterprises. This research was collected through surveys, questionnaires, and personal interviews via direct mail, in-person and Web site collection, e-mail, and telephone conversations. Outreach to potential respondents was facilitated through the generous assistance of the USC Career Planning & Placement Center, USC Lambda Alumni Association, gay.com, gfn.com, National Gay and Lesbian Business Conference, planetout.com, ReachingOut MBA, and the author's personal contacts developed through professional associations and his own leadership role at the University of Southern California.

Research Steps

The research breaks down into four major phases:

1. GLBT (Gay, Lesbian, Bisexual, Transgender) Professionals (2000–2004)

- *2000–2001:* A survey instrument collected quantitative data about the career experiences of 302 gay, lesbian, bisexual, and transgender alumni from the University of Southern California, representing diverse fields and industries.

- *2001–2003:* Personal interviews collected qualitative data from a subset of the 302 alumni about their individual career experiences.
- *2003–2004:* A revised survey instrument collected additional data about the career experiences of 1,205 gay, lesbian, bisexual, and transgender professionals across the country, representing diverse fields and industries.

2. Recruiters, Hiring Managers (2003–2004)

- *Survey 1:* A survey instrument collected data from 530 recruiters and hiring managers, primarily from Fortune 500 companies, about desirable principles identified as contributing to leadership success over the next ten years. Specific principles included diversity, creativity, and emotional intelligence.
- *Survey 2:* A survey instrument collected data from 244 recruiters, hiring managers, and gay managers about employee engagement across different business sectors (Fortune 500 companies, colleges and universities, government and nonprofit, and entrepreneurial and owner-run).

3. Employees of Gay Executives (2004–2005)

A survey instrument collected quantitative data about the employee experiences of 1,048 employees reporting to gay managers across these same four sectors (Fortune 500 companies, colleges and universities, government and nonprofit, and entrepreneurial and owner-run).

4. G Quotient Leadership (2005)

Based on the seven identified principles of G Quotient leadership, a questionnaire was developed consisting of fifty-two statements reflecting beliefs and behaviors associated with these same principles. The responses of 220 managers (straight women, lesbians, straight men, and gay men) were measured for both consistency and content and led to the development of the G Quotient Assessment featured in this book. This population represented managers across the same four business sectors (Fortune 500, colleges and universities, government and nonprofit, and entrepreneurial and owner-run).

Subsequently, gay managers from the following companies and organizations participated in personal interviews, providing detailed, qualitative data about their leadership beliefs and behaviors as featured throughout this book:

- A.T. Kearney
- Bain & Company
- Barclay's Bank
- Citicorp
- Deloitte Consulting LLP
- Disney
- Ernst & Young
- General Electric
- Hampshire College
- IBM
- State of Massachusetts
- Mitchell Gold + Bob Williams
- Morgan Stanley
- PepsiCo
- Quest Diagnostics
- Replacements, Inc.
- University of California
- University of Southern California

APPENDIX C

ASSESSMENT RESEARCH

Table One

Descriptive Statistics: G Quotient Assessment Survey Scores

Straight Females

	Number	Minimum Score	Maximum Score	Average Score	Std. Deviation
GQ	28	68.00	116.00	93.2500	13.5089

Lesbians

	Number	Minimum Score	Maximum Score	Average Score	Std. Deviation
GQ	28	74.00	123.00	101.6786	9.0392

Straight Men

	Number	Minimum Score	Maximum Score	Average Score	Std. Deviation
GQ	48	61.00	119.00	80.0208	14.6018

Gay Men

	Number	Minimum Score	Maximum Score	Average Score	Std. Deviation
GQ	116	61.00	124.00	110.5000	11.7943

Table Two

Responses by gender and sexual orientation to the twenty-five final G Quotient assessment statements.

1. I do not believe that my organization or business can reach full potential without the input and participation of all employees.

	Straight Females	Lesbians	Straight Males	Gay Males
Never	0	3.6	6.3	3.4
Seldom	0	3.6	6.3	0.9
Sometimes	17.9	3.6	14.6	1.7
Frequently	46.4	32.1	62.5	19
Always	35.7	57.1	10.4	75

2. A key to my management style is discerning my employees' motivational pathways.

	Straight Females	Lesbians	Straight Males	Gay Males
Never	3.6	0	0	0
Seldom	3.6	0	0	0
Sometimes	25	3.6	60.4	6
Frequently	53.6	60.7	33.3	29.3
Always	14.3	35.7	6.3	64.7

3. I depend upon my employees for new ways of accomplishing tasks and meeting goals.

	Straight Females	Lesbians	Straight Males	Gay Males
Never	0	0	0	0
Seldom	0	3.6	8.3	1.7
Sometimes	35.7	14.3	54.2	8.7
Frequently	53.6	46.4	27.1	34.8
Always	10.7	35.7	10.4	54.8

4. I believe that changing the organization or business environment to help employees with the practical aspects of life is critical.

	Straight Females	Lesbians	Straight Males	Gay Males
Never	3.6	0	0	0.9
Seldom	10.7	3.6	31.3	0
Sometimes	46.4	7.1	56.3	6
Frequently	32.1	39.3	6.3	37.1
Always	7.1	50	6.3	56

5. I don't get much back from the energy that I put into professional relationships.

	Straight Females	Lesbians	Straight Males	Gay Males
Never	14.3	14.3	12.5	39.7
Seldom	42.9	42.9	39.6	43.1
Sometimes	25	39.3	39.6	10.3
Frequently	14.3	3.6	8.3	6
Always	3.6	0	0	0.9

6. My actions to facilitate an employee's growth and development improve the work environment.

	Straight Females	Lesbians	Straight Males	Gay Males
Never	0	0	0	0.9
Seldom	0	0	8.3	0.9
Sometimes	35.7	3.6	68.3	4.3
Frequently	39.3	46.4	8.3	22.6
Always	25	50	14.6	71.3

7. The contacts that I have with others in leadership roles facilitate my success.

	Straight Females	Lesbians	Straight Males	Gay Males
Never	0	0	0	0.9
Seldom	17.9	3.6	8.3	3.5
Sometimes	17.9	32.1	50	9.6
Frequently	46.4	28.6	29.2	39.1
Always	17.9	35.7	12.5	47

8. My role as manager or supervisor, while important, is not superior in value to the roles of those in my employ.

	Straight Females	Lesbians	Straight Males	Gay Males
Never	3.6	0	18.8	2.6
Seldom	17.9	10.7	33.3	3.5
Sometimes	39.3	21.4	35.4	2.6
Frequently	14.3	39.3	8.3	22.8
Always	25	28.6	4.2	68.4

9. I rely upon brainstorming with my employees for new concepts that give our organization or business the edge.

	Straight Females	Lesbians	Straight Males	Gay Males
Never	0	0	0	0
Seldom	0	0	20.8	0.9
Sometimes	50	28.6	54.2	7.8
Frequently	25	50	22.9	36.2
Always	25	21.4	2.1	55.2

10. Losing a good employee to a promotion is frequently detrimental to the organization or business financially, as well as a drain on my energy.

	Straight Females	Lesbians	Straight Males	Gay Males
Never	17.9	39.3	4.2	53.4
Seldom	32.1	35.7	29.2	36.2
Sometimes	39.3	17.9	33.3	6.9
Frequently	10.7	3.6	25	2.6
Always	0	3.6	8.3	0.9

11. I believe it is important to be able to recognize and make use of the talents my employees have.

	Straight Females	Lesbians	Straight Males	Gay Males
Never	0	0	0	0
Seldom	0	0	0	0
Sometimes	10.7	0	22.9	0
Frequently	35.7	25	47.9	11.2
Always	53.6	75	29.2	88.8

12. It is important to me that all my employees know that I value and respect them all equally well.

	Straight Females	Lesbians	Straight Males	Gay Males
Never	0	0	0	0
Seldom	0	0	4.2	0
Sometimes	14.3	3.6	37.5	2.6
Frequently	21.4	21.4	33.3	7.8
Always	64.3	75	25	89.7

13. I have discovered that when the process of working together is enjoyable, the work gets done.

	Straight Females	Lesbians	Straight Males	Gay Males
Never	0	0	0	0
Seldom	0	0	12.5	0.9
Sometimes	35.7	7.1	64.6	1.7
Frequently	42.9	46.4	12.5	29.3
Always	21.4	46.4	10.4	68.1

14. I enjoy keeping my organization or business on the move and adapting to the times.

	Straight Females	Lesbians	Straight Males	Gay Males
Never	0	0	0	0
Seldom	0	0	2.1	1.7
Sometimes	32.1	10.7	68.8	2.6
Frequently	35.7	50	22.9	28.4
Always	32.1	39.3	6.3	67.2

15. Too much energy is spent adapting to changes in my organization or business that can be done without.

	Straight Females	Lesbians	Straight Males	Gay Males
Never	7.1	17.9	6.3	35.1
Seldom	32.1	32.1	10.4	50.9
Sometimes	60.7	39.3	64.6	9.6
Frequently	0	7.1	18.8	3.5
Always	0	3.6	0	0.9

16. I find that diverse populations result in diverse talents and skills, all of which are important for the success of my organization or business.

	Straight Females	Lesbians	Straight Males	Gay Males
Never	0	0	0	0.9
Seldom	7.1	3.6	10.4	0
Sometimes	28.6	3.6	66.7	5.2
Frequently	39.3	28.6	16.7	11.3
Always	25	64.3	6.3	82.6

17. When things are not going well in my organization or business, I look for organizational failures rather than individual failures.

	Straight Females	Lesbians	Straight Males	Gay Males
Never	0	0	0	0.9
Seldom	7.4	0	12.5	2.6
Sometimes	59.3	21.4	70.8	15.7
Frequently	25.9	67.9	16.7	39.1
Always	7.4	10.7	0	41.7

18. When my employees contribute to the innovation within the organization or business, they feel connected and valued.

	Straight Females	Lesbians	Straight Males	Gay Males
Never	0	0	0	0
Seldom	0	0	2.1	0.9
Sometimes	17.9	3.6	54.2	0.9
Frequently	53.6	39.3	33.3	20.2
Always	28.6	57.1	10.4	78.1

19. I find that I am able to spot a good deal without necessarily hearing all the facts.

	Straight Females	Lesbians	Straight Males	Gay Males
Never	0	7.1	0	0
Seldom	7.1	14.3	10.4	6
Sometimes	39.3	46.4	81.3	18.1
Frequently	50	32.1	6.3	35.3
Always	3.6	0	2.1	40.5

20. It is important not to lean upon hunches as a manager but trust only in the facts.

	Straight Females	Lesbians	Straight Males	Gay Males
Never	0	0	0	9.6
Seldom	25	21.4	12.5	46.5
Sometimes	53.6	60.7	18.8	37.7
Frequently	17.9	14.3	37.5	5.3
Always	3.6	3.6	31.3	0.9

21. My ability to bring out the best in my employees comes from my ability to see and understand their needs and wants.

	Straight Females	Lesbians	Straight Males	Gay Males
Never	0	0	4.2	1.8
Seldom	0	0	10.4	0.9
Sometimes	39.3	7.1	58.3	5.3
Frequently	35.7	57.1	22.9	28.1
Always	25	35.7	4.2	64

22. As a manager I have a knack for putting people together in ways that result in successful working relationships.

	Straight Females	Lesbians	Straight Males	Gay Males
Never	0	0	0	0
Seldom	0	0	4.2	0
Sometimes	42.9	50	75	7.1
Frequently	53.6	39.3	10.4	34.5
Always	3.6	10.7	10.4	58.4

23. I want to see all employees aspire to and attain higher positions.

	Straight Females	Lesbians	Straight Males	Gay Males
Never	0	0	0	0
Seldom	3.6	0	18.8	0
Sometimes	25	10.7	41.7	7
Frequently	35.7	46.4	27.1	20.2
Always	35.7	42.9	12.5	72.8

24. Justice and equity in the treatment of employees is one of my basic rules.

	Straight Females	Lesbians	Straight Males	Gay Males
Never	0	0	0	0
Seldom	0	0	2.1	0.9
Sometimes	14.3	0	29.2	0.9
Frequently	42.9	25	54.2	5.3
Always	42.9	75	14.6	93

25. I believe that my organization or business runs smoothest
using tried-and-true processes and procedures.

	Straight Females	Lesbians	Straight Males	Gay Males
Never	0	3.6	0	20.2
Seldom	17.9	17.9	6.3	44.7
Sometimes	53.6	50	18.8	28.1
Frequently	28.6	25	43.8	5.3
Always	0	3.6	31.3	1.8

APPENDIX D

EMPLOYEE SURVEY

Employees Reporting to Gay Managers

Total: 1,048

Sex:
626 Women
406 Men
 16 No Answer

Age Range: 21–72

Average Age: 41 (40.907)

Field or Industry:
158 Education
 56 Entrepreneur
658 Fortune 500
 54 Government or Nonprofit
122 No Answer

States:
  1 Hawaii
  1 Nebraska

1   South Carolina

1   Wisconsin

3   Arizona

3   Indiana

4   Nevada

5   Maryland

7   Minnesota

7   Pennsylvania

8   Colorado

9   Michigan

10   Virginia

11   Texas

12   New Jersey

14   Georgia

15   Oregon

20   District of Columbia

26   Washington

30   Massachusetts

31   Florida

31   Illinois

40   New York

702   California

47   No Answer

Outside the United States

1   England

2   China

2   Switzerland

4   Canada

Note: Responses to the following statements are reported in percentages for male and female employees combined.

1. I am satisfied with my job:

   Yes 81.39%; No 15.26%; No Answer 3.33%

2. Morale in my working unit is high:

   Yes 84.82%; No 13.26%; No Answer 1.90%

3. I always do my best to perform excellent work:

   Yes 85.30%; No 12.02%; No Answer 2.67%

4. I trust my manager to advocate for my best interest within the company or organization:

   Yes 80.24%; No 15.74%; No Answer 4.00%

5. I am always treated fairly by my manager:

   Yes 84.35%; No 11.92%; No Answer 3.81%

6. My manager treats other employees fairly in my working unit:

   Yes 85.30%; No 11.35%; No Answer 3.33%

7. My manager's policies for promotion and advancement are fair:

   Yes 80.62%; No 16.31%; No Answer 3.05%

8. I respect my manager as a professional:

   Yes 86.16%; No 10.78%; No Answer 3.05%

9. My manager demonstrates strong leadership skills:

   Yes 86.83%; No 10.49%; No Answer 2.67%

10. Information and knowledge is shared openly within my working unit:

    Yes 91.41%; No 5.72%; No Answer 2.86%

11. Communication between employees is encouraged in my working unit:

    Yes 91.22%; No 5.53%; No Answer 3.24%

12. Creativity is encouraged by my manager in my working unit:

   Yes 87.40%; No 9.73%; No Answer 2.86%

13. People who challenge the status quo are valued in my working unit:

   Yes 85.78%; No 10.59%; No Answer 3.62%

14. I can disagree with my manager without being afraid of getting in trouble:

   Yes 88.93%; No 8.39%; No Answer 2.67%

15. People with different ideas are valued in my working unit:

   Yes 85.40%; No 11.25%; No Answer 3.33%

16. I believe my ideas and opinions matter to my manager:

   Yes 86.73%; No 10.20%; No Answer 2.95%

Notes

Preface

1. This information comes from a 2005 Towers Perrin study of more than 85,000 people working for large and midsize companies in sixteen different countries across four continents. It is cited in a Towers Perrin news release published on Business Wire, November 15, 2005: "Largest Single Study of the Workforce Worldwide Shows That Employee Engagement Levels Pose a Threat to Corporate Performance Globally." This information is consistent with findings of the 2005 Employee/Employer Equation Survey conducted by Harris Interactive, Inc., which included responses from a nationwide sample of 7,718 American employees aged eighteen and over and found that only 20 percent of American employees report feeling passionate or "engaged" in their jobs.
2. This information also comes from the 2005 Employee/Employer Equation Survey.
3. This information comes from the 2005 Randstad report, 2005 Employee Review. The report cites a drop from 44 percent in 2004 to 40 percent in 2005 for U.S. workers who rate morale "good" to "excellent."

Introduction

1. Human Rights Campaign Foundation, "Corporate Equality Index 2005." Available online: www.hrc.org. Access date: February 8, 2006.

2. Daniel McGinn, "Fresh Ideas," *Newsweek,* June 13, 2005.

3. See Simba Information, "Business of Consumer Book Publishing," 2004.

4. J. M. Andriote, *Victory Deferred: How AIDS Changed Gay Life in America* (Chicago: University of Chicago Press, 1999), pp. 19–20.

5. W. Odets, "Some Thoughts on Gay Male Relationships and American Society," *Journal of the Gay and Lesbian Medical Association,* Fall 1998, 2(1); W. Odets, *In the Shadow of the Epidemic: Being HIV-Negative in the Age of AIDS* (Durham, N.C.: Duke University Press), 1995.

6. M. Gladwell, *Blink: The Power of Thinking Without Thinking* (New York: Little Brown, 2005).

7. This information is from a summary of *The New Female Entrepreneur* (2005), by William Walstad and Marilyn Kourilsky, as it appears in the Fall 2005 issue of *Nebraska Business,* a publication of the University of Nebraska.

8. The source for this information is a 1990 *Library Journal* review written by James Van Buskirk for *Hidden From History,* by Martin Duberman, Plume Books, 1990. The information is available on Amazon.com in the review section for Duberman's book.

9. E. Hooker, "The Adjustment of the Male Overt Homosexual," *Journal of Projective Techniques,* 1957, *21,* 18–31.

10. Andriote, 1999, p. 31.

11. M. Duberman, M. Vicinus, and G. Chauncey, *Hidden from History: Reclaiming the Gay and Lesbian Past* (New York: Plume Books, 1990).

12. J. D. Mayer, D. R. Caruso, and P. Salovey, "Emotional Intelligence Meets Traditional Standards for an Intelligence," *Intelligence,* 2000, *27,* 267.

Chapter 1

1. L. Iacocca, "Henry Ford," *Time,* December 7, 1998.

2. See "Money Talks, but Employees Walk for Other Reasons," September 14, 2005. Available online: www.hudson-index.com. Access date: February 7, 2006.
3. D. McClelland, *The Achieving Society* (New York: Free Press, 1967).
4. "Most Employees Not Engaged at Work," May 2, 2005. Available online: www.workindex.com. Access date: February 7, 2006.
5. "Money Talks, but Not That Loud," *Work & Family Newsbrief*, October 2005. Available online (with free subscription): www.workfamily.com. This newsletter is a monthly eight-page digest of the nation's most important work-life news about best practices, research, company experiences, legislation and partnerships. The editors go through thousands of publications and summarize various news items for a quick and easy read.
6. See "Twain's Notebook, 1902–1903." Available online: www.twainquotes.com. Access date: February 7, 2006.

Chapter 2

1. R. Florida, *Rise of the Creative Class*, Reprint Ed. (New York: Basic Books, 2004).
2. S. Gryskiewicz, "Cashing in on Creativity at Work—the Importance, Definition, and Encouragement of Business Creativity," *Psychology Today*, September/October 2000, pp. 63–65.
3. Gryskiewicz, 2000.
4. W. Bennis and P. Ward-Biderman, *Organizing Genius: The Secrets of Creative Collaboration* (Reading, Mass.: Addison-Wesley, 1997), p. xvi.
5. This information is cited in a January 1999 speech given by Gay Mitchell, Executive Vice-President of the Royal Bank of Canada, at McMaster University's 2nd World Congress on Management of Intellectual Capital. The quote can be accessed at www.leadershipnow.com/creativityquotes.html. Access date: February 27, 2006.

6. M. DePree, *Leadership Is an Art*, Reissue Ed. (New York: Dell, 1990).

Chapter 3

1. See A. Toffler, *The Third Wave*, Reissue Ed. (New York: Bantam, 1984), and A. Toffler, *Future Shock*, Reissue Ed. (New York: Bantam, 1984).
2. C. Dickens, *Martin Chuzzlewit* (New York: Penguin Classics, 2000), Chapter 18. (Originally published 1844.)

Chapter 4

1. Aristotle, *Nicomachean Ethics*, 2nd ed., translated by Terence Irwin (Indianapolis, Ind.: Hackett, 2000), Book 8, pp. 200–227.
2. M. Gladwell, *The Tipping Point* (New York: Back Bay Books, 2002), pp. 46, 51.

Chapter 5

1. "Perceptions on Ethics," *HR Magazine*, November 2004.
2. K. Snyder, *Lavender Road to Success* (Berkeley, Calif.: Ten Speed Press, 2003).
3. "Perceptions on Ethics," 2004. The article cites the poll findings of a study conducted by the Society for Human Resource Management and CareerJournal.com.
4. M. W. Seeger, *Organizational Communication Ethics: Decisions and Dilemmas* (Cresskill, N.J.: Hampton Press, 1997), pp. 187–188.
5. H. D. Thoreau, *Walden* (New York: Dover, 1995), p. 107. (Originally published 1854.)

Chapter 6

1. M. Sinclair and N. M. Ashkanasy, "Intuition: Myth or a Decision-Making Tool?" *ManagementLearning*, 2005, 36(3), 353–370.
2. Sinclair and Ashkanasy, 2005.

3. J. Dewey, *Experience and Nature* (La Salle, Ill.: Open Court, 1925), p. 244.

4. C. G., Jung, G. Adler, and R. Hull, *Collected Works of C. G. Jung* (Princeton, N.J.: Bollingen, 1979).

5. *Merriam-Webster's Collegiate Dictionary*, 11th Ed. (Springfield, Mass.: Merriam-Webster, 2004).

6. F. Korthagen, "The Organization in Balance: Reflection and Intuition as Complementary Processes," *Management Learning*, 2005, 36(3), 371–387.

7. F. Smith, "Golden Gut," Forbes Magazine Web Exclusive, September 7, 2002. Available online: www.forbes.com/asap/2002/1007/Hunches.html. Access date: February 27, 2006.

Chapter 7

1. "Companies Risk Greater Employee Turnover and Lower Productivity Without Improved Teamwork," *Business Wire*, July 6, 2005. Available online: www.haygroup.com/ww/Media/press_releases.asp (search on "Organizational Effectiveness"). Access date: February 27, 2006.

2. "Companies Risk . . . " 2005.

3. *Merriam-Webster's Collegiate Dictionary* (11th Ed.), Springfield, Mass.: Merriam-Webster, 2004.

4. W. S. Pollack, " 'Masked Men': New Psychoanalytically Oriented Treatment Models for Adult and Young Adult Men," in G. Brooks and G. Good (Eds.), *The New Handbook of Psychotherapy and Counseling for Men* (Vol. 2) (San Francisco: Jossey-Bass, 2001), pp. 527–543.

Chapter 8

1. S. Crabtree, "Getting Personal in the Workplace," *Gallup Management Journal*, June 10, 2004.

2. "U.S. Job Satisfaction Keeps Falling, Conference Board Reports Today," The Conference Board, February 28, 2005. Available

online: www.conference-board.org. Access date: February 7, 2006.

3. Towers Perrin, "Largest Single Study of the Workforce World-wide Shows That Employee Engagement Levels Pose a Threat to Corporate Performance Globally," November 15, 2005. Available online: www.towersperrin.com (go to HR Services and search on "Largest Single Study"). Access date: February 27, 2006.

4. "U.S. Middle Managers' Satisfaction with Employers Drops, Accenture Survey Finds; Believe Companies Are Mismanaged, See Few Prospects for Advancement," *Business Wire*, October 20, 2005. Available online: http://findarticles.com/ (search on title). Access date: February 27, 2006.

5. A. J. Meadows, "Craft an Effective Message to Support Diversity," *DiversityInc.*, October/November 2004, p. 62.

6. "Diversity Officer Special Report," Washington, D.C.: Diversity Best Practices, September 30, 2004.

7. David A. Carter, Betty J. Simkins, and W. Gary Simpson, "Corporate Governance, Board Diversity and Firm Value," *Financial Review*, 2003, 38(1), 33.

8. Quoted at www.amazon.com, in the Review section for J. Jacobs, *The Economy of Cities* (New York: Vintage, 1969).

9. S. Sassen, *Cities in a World Economy* (London: Sage, 1994), and P. Bairoch, *Cities and Economic Development: From the Dawn of History to the Present* (Oxford, England: Oxford University Press, 1988).

10. G.-J. Hospers, "Jane Jacobs: Her Life and Work," Preservation Institute, n.d. Available online: http://www.preservenet.com/studies/Jacobsbio.html. Access date: February 7, 2006.

11. J. Quigley, CEO of Deloitte & Touche LLP, "Diversity—from Compliance to Competitive Advantage," speech at the Commonwealth Club, San Francisco, California, April 22, 2004.

12. R. Levering and M. Moskowitz, *The 100 Best Companies to Work for in America*, Rev. Ed. (Reading, Mass.: Addison-Wesley, 1993).

13. SAP and Accenture, "Human Capital Management: Managing and Maximizing People to Achieve High Performance," a White Paper Report, 2005. Available online: www.sap.com/ (search on title). Access date: February 27, 2006.

14. M. Lillich, "Marketing Prof's Research Links Employee Satisfaction, Profits," *Krannert Magazine* (Purdue University), 2005, 6(2).

15. R. Inglehart, "Globalization and Postmodern Values," *Washington Quarterly*, Winter 2000.

16. "A New Kind of Company," *Newsweek International Edition*, July 4, 2005; "Ratan Tata: No One's Doubting Now," *Business Week*, July 26, 2004.

17. "A New Kind of Company," 2005; "Ratan Tata: No One's Doubting Now," 2004.

18. "Ratan N. Tata: Linking Shareholder Value and Social Responsibility," *Global Giving Matters*, February-April 2005.

19. R. Florida, *Rise of the Creative Class*, Reprint Ed. (New York: Basic Books, 2004), p. 91.

20. U. Kher/Rochester, "Getting Kodak to Focus," *Time*, February 14, 2005; D. Lidor, "Kodak's Image Takes Shape," *Forbes*, August 25, 2005.

21. D. McGregor, *The Human Side of Enterprise* (New York: McGraw-Hill, 1960).

22. R. E. Mittelstaedt Jr., *Will Your Next Mistake Be Fatal?* (Upper Saddle River, N.J.: Wharton School of Publishing, 2005). Some information in this paragraph comes from a review and analysis of the book in the *Wharton Alumni Magazine*, Winter 2005.

23. J. Collins, *Good to Great* (New York: HarperCollins, 2001), p. 125.

24. M. Dittman, "Happy Employees Make Happy Families, Study Finds," *Monitor on Psychology*, 2005, 36(4), 23.

Chapter 9

1. A. Watts and A. C. Huang, *Tao: The Watercourse Way* (New York: Pantheon Books, 1975).

2. D. Kolb, *Experiential Learning* (New York: Prentice-Hall, 1984).

3. E. McCulloch-Lovell, "A Vocation of the Imagination," *Connection: New England's Journal of Higher Education*, Summer 2005. Available online: www.findarticles.com/ (search on title). Access date: February 17, 2006.

4. Information on the Chicago Innovation Awards is available online: www.chicagoinnovationawards.com. Access date: February 7, 2006.

5. T. Kucamarski, "Award Winners Find Innovation Profitable," *Chicago Sun Times*, June 16, 2005.

6. M.E.P. Seligman and M. Csikszentmihalyi, "Positive Psychology: An Introduction," *American Psychologist*, 2000, 55(1), 5–14.

7. M. Seligman, T. Steen, N. Park, and C. Peterson, "Positive Psychology Progress," *American Psychologist*, July-August 2005, p. 410.

8. G. Williams, "Living the Dream: Small Wonders: Small Businesses Make Big Impacts When They Keep Innovation in Mind," *Entrepreneur Magazine*, May 2005.

Chapter 10

1. R. Florida, *Rise of the Creative Class*, Reprint Ed. (New York: Basic Books, 2004).

Chapter 11

1. S. Holtz, "Establishing Connections: Today's Communication Technologies Have Shifted the Dynamic, Opening a Dialogue Between Senders and Receivers," *Communication World*, May-June 2005.

2. "Internet World Stats News," June 2005. Available online: www.internetworldstats.com. Access date: February 7, 2006.

3. "March 2005 Bandwidth Report." Available online: www.websiteoptimization.com/bw/0503/. Access date: February 17,

2006. The data is based on information derived from Nielsen/ NetRatings reports.

4. "Mobile Entertainment: The Rise of the Very Small Screen," eMarketer, January 1, 2006.

5. "Podcast Projections," *eMarketer*, November 18, 2005.

6. J. Challenger, "Embracing Today's Global Economy," *USA Today* magazine (published by the Society for the Advancement of Education), September 2005.

7. W. J. Holstein, "The Sixth Annual CEO Leadership Summit: Global Forces Are Transforming the U.S. Economy," *Chief Executive*, January-February 2005.

8. R. Leong, "Global Economy—Manufacturing Grows in 2005 but Losing Momentum," Reuters, January 3, 2006.

9. E. Chester, *Employing Generation Why?* (Colorado: Tucker House Books, 2002), p. 13.

10. S. Armour, "Generation Y: They've Arrived at Work with a New Attitude," *USA Today*, November 6, 2005.

11. P. Allen, "Why and How: Managing Different Generations in the Workplace," *Benefits Canada*, September 2004.

12. Armour, 2005.

13. "Motivating Generation Y," *Management News Issues*, November 10, 2003. Available online: www.management-issues.com/ display_page.asp?section=research&id=974. Access date: February 17, 2006.

14. MIT Communications Forum, April 1, 2004. Transcripts available online: http://web.mit.edu/comm-forum/forums/changing_audiences.html. Access date: February 7, 2006.

15. "Coming of Age in America, Part II," GQR+*Polimetrix Youth Monitor*, October 2005. Available online: www.greenbergresearch .com. Access date: February 7, 2006.

16. Cooperative Institutional Research Program (CIRP), "2004 Annual Freshman Survey Report." Los Angeles: Higher Education Research Institute (HERI), UCLA. This survey is completed by 289,452 students from 440 institutions across the nation.

Acknowledgments

Like all worthwhile and rewarding projects in life, this book reflects the collaborative efforts of a great number of exceptional people. My deepest gratitude goes to my family and friends, who have encouraged me and cheered me on from the beginning of this project. I'm looking forward to spending endless hours enjoying your wonderful company without being attached to a laptop or notebook! Included in my family is my partner, Kirwan Rockefeller. Thank you for always being there to support my work and for making it (and me) so much better.

Throughout these past five years, I have had the good fortune to be assisted in my efforts to reach out to many diverse populations in order to make my research and this book possible. Particularly, I would like to thank Eileen Kohan and Angie Wood at the USC Career Planning & Placement Center, the leaders and members of the USC Lambda Alumni Association, Walter B. Schubert Jr. and Cory Calvin at gfn.com, Julie Ross at PlanetOut Partners (planetout.com and gay.com), and Jaime Singson, Ian Tzeng, and all the dedicated organizers of the 2005 Reaching Out MBA conference. Thank you for making my work possible.

One of the best decisions I have ever made was to work with my talented agent Felicia Eth. Thank you for always being honest and recognizing where this project was headed even when I was unsure of its ultimate direction. I will forever appreciate your being in my corner. The collaborative effort that led to this book is most evident when it comes to my publisher Jossey-Bass. I would first like to thank my executive editor, Susan Williams, for taking such wonderful care of this project and shepherding it through all its incarnations. Thank you for recognizing the value of *The G Quotient*. To Byron Schneider, thank you for maximizing my material. You helped me say everything in just the right way. Also, many thanks to Rob Brandt for all of your advice and guidance throughout this project, and to the president of Jossey-Bass, Debra Hunter, for allowing me to become part of this exceptional group of professionals.

A big thanks to Scott Lewallen at mezic.com for being a creative and technical wizard! I greatly appreciate all your technological guidance. Finally, I would like to acknowledge all my past and present students at the University of Southern California. You inspire me on a daily basis and I cannot think of any greater professional reward than to be teaching at my own alma mater, particularly in the Marshall School of Business. I have great faith in the future because of all of you.

The Author

KIRK SNYDER is nationally recognized as an expert in the field of career development and the study of work in contemporary society. At the University of Southern California, he teaches business communication in the Marshall School of Business. He also heads his own consulting firm, Equality Career Group, Inc. In addition to his current USC role, he has held several senior-level leadership positions in the field of higher education as well as teaching theories of career development for six years in the USC Rossier School of Education.

As an author, researcher, and educator, Snyder has generated attention from many of the world's most prestigious publications, including the *New York Times*, *Chicago Tribune*, *Miami Herald*, *Atlanta Journal-Constitution*, and *The Advocate*. His 2003 debut book, *Lavender Road to Success*, was named by Amazon.com as one of the best books of the year as a top ten editors' pick. He lives in Southern California.

Index

Communication: with authenticity and truth, 61–63, 66; benefits of direct, 70–71; "emoticon" symbols used as part of, 57; engaging your employees with effective, 59–60; ethics in, 67–72; global marketplace and role of, 72; of individual value of employees, 71–72; Johari Window model of, 110; organization honesty in management, practices, 68–72

Communication principle: ethics as part of, 67–72; implemented at A.T. Kearney, 64–67; implemented by Barclays Global Investors, 68–72; importance of being heard as part of, 63–64; Jarrett Barrios's implementation of, 61–63

Communication World, 149

Concepts (creativity), 22

Connectivity: creating tribal knowledge through, 55–57; exploring concept of, 48–50; external networking, 47; of gay men's networks, 49–50; and internal awareness, 47–48

Connectivity principle: Citi-Capital implementation of, 50–52; creating meaning through, 52–53; University of California implementation of, 53–55

"Connectors," 55

Cooperative Institutional Research Program, 156

Copyright registrations, 130

Cousins, N., 52

Crate & Barrel, 7

Creativity: becoming inspired by, 30–31; bridging innovation and, 28–30; confidence required for, 33; G Quotient environment context of, 21–22, 26, 30; managing, 26–28; standing apart through, 32–34; turned into innovation, 23

Creativity principle: Bain & Company's implementa-

tion of, 28–30, 142–143; concepts, possibilities, and people focus of, 22–23; Hampshire College's implementation of, 24–26; IBM Global Services' implementation of, 32–34

Cultural differences, 13

Daewoo Motors, 111

Deloitte & Touche USA LLP, 37, 106

Deloitte Career Connections, 107

Deloitte Consulting, 37–39

DeMille, C. B., 53

DePree, M., 30

Dewey, J., 74–75

Dickens, C., 43

Digital Age: changing context of life in the, 151; communication techniques of the, 60; Eastman Kodak's strategy for entering the, 112–113; information availability through, 125; information of, 60, 62, 125; Internet as information source in the, 149–150; reflection and intuition as currency of, 79; taking us beyond the, 159; using truth to communicate in the, 62

Direct communication, 70–71

Disney, R., 74

Disney, W., 73–74, 78

Disneyland, 73–74

Diversity: GLBT, 15–16, 32–33, 42, 81; how G Quotient leadership facilitates, 119–120; learning to appreciate benefits of, 119–120

Diversity Best Practices survey, 104

Diversity Inc.'s top fifty companies list, 103

"Don Quixote" syndrome, 45

Donne, J., 48

Douglas, Lord A., 135

Drucker, P., 111

Eastman Kodak Company, 112–113

Economy of Cities, The (Jacobs), 105

Edwards, J., 150

Einstein, A., 84

eMarketer, 150

"Emoticon" symbols, 57

Employee blame cycle, 133–134

Employee engagement: collaboration contributions to, 86–87, 92; creative opportunities for, 26; effective communication to facilitate, 59–60; experiential learning linked to, 125–126; inclusion to invite, 15–17; job ownership element of, 115–117, 135; low levels of U.S., 101–102

Employee-management relationships: connectivity as part of, 51–52; inclusion principle's impact on, 9–10, 14–15; trust element of, 60–61, 68, 93–97

Employees: accessing intellectual capital of, 90; average work week of, 108–109; balancing needs of organizations, customers, and, 121–122; collaboration with, 85–97; Comfort Zone at Mitchell Gold + Bob Williams created for, 7–8; creating meaning through connectivity, 52–53; developing potential of, 66–67; feedback on G Quotient environment by, 116–117, 138–147; focus on positive characteristics of, 133–134; G Quotient leadership's respect and value of, 4; Gen X, 102; Gen Y, 52, 101, 102, 153–157; happiness matters to, 108–110; importance of being heard to, 63–64; inclusion as promoting motivation of, 8–14; increasing concerns over erosion of trust by, 68; individual value of, 37, 71–72; job ownership by,

11303612R00137

Made in the USA
San Bernardino, CA
21 May 2014